DO-IT-YOURSELF YEARBOOK

WEEKEND HOME PROJECTS

NORTH COAST PRODUCTIONS
ST. PAUL, MINNESOTA

A NORTH COAST PUBLICATION
Published by North Coast Productions
2136 Ford Parkway, Box 355
St. Paul, MN 55116

Gene Schnaser, Editor and Publisher
Jeanne Fredensborg, Managing Editor
Merle Henkenius, Contributing Editor
Paul Butler, Contributing Editor
Marya Butler, Contributing Artist
Marlyn Rodi, Contributing Artist

The editors of this book are dedicated to presenting information and ideas needed to successfully plan and execute do-it-yourself activities. If you have any comments or suggestions, please address your correspondence to the address above. Also use the address above for inquiries regarding special editions of this book, for reprints of features, photography, or artwork, or for use of this book's content in electronic media.

A very special thanks to the many people, companies, and organizations who assisted the staff, either directly or indirectly, in making this book a reality. For their valuable editorial advice the editors wish to thank Jim Fassel, Russ Barnard, Gene Ohman, Mark Lambie, Ron A. Bruzek, Mark Newhall, Marlyn Rodi, and Harold M. Johnson. For their valuable help in getting this book to the reader: Judy Holby, Shane Dennis, Alan Tsai, and David H. Li.

Note To The Reader: The information, plans, and instructions in this book have come from a variety of sources. Every effort has been made to ensure the accuracy of data presented. However, due to differing conditions, tools, and individual skills, the publisher and the staff cannot assume responsibility for any injuries suffered, damages, or losses incurred during or as a result of following this information. Before beginning any project, it is important to consider personal safety above all else. Review the plans and procedures carefully and, if any doubts or questions remain concerning your personal safety, working procedures, or use of materials, consult local experts or authorities. Also, always read and observe all of the safety precautions provided by any tool, equipment, or materials manufacturer, and always follow all accepted safety procedures.

PREFACE

A Do-It-Yourself Bonanza

We are proud to bring you this brand-new package of information that will not only help you improve and maintain your home in the years ahead, but also will give you dozens of ideas for projects that you can accomplish in a single weekend. Whether you are a beginning do-it-yourselfer or an old hand, the advice on the following pages will tell you how to get these projects done, step by step.

For example, you will see how to make valuable repairs throughout your home, including how to keep a driveway in good shape, how to make critical repairs on damaged shingles, how to repair broken ceramic tiles, how to fix tattered wall corners, how to make quick repairs on wallpaper, how to troubleshoot problems with switches, and more.

Inside this book you will also see how to make major improvements to your home, including how to set up a home workshop. You will see how to build split-block retaining walls, how to overhaul your time-worn bathroom, how to replace your kitchen's outdated plumbing, how to upgrade your laundry room's vent system, how to add dimmer switches to your fluorescent fixtures, along with other projects that will protect your home investment.

Besides showing you some great ideas on how to plan and set up a home workshop, we have included tips on buying the tools that will make your do-it-yourself projects easier. As a bonus, a special section provides spaces for you to keep a full record of your personal tool inventory. And, to help you hone your do-it-yourself skills, we present two in-depth articles on the techniques of using wood glues and making measurements in your project work.

In addition to all this, we have also included how to build great shelving for your home, plus a dozen other fun projects that you can build in a weekend. Each of these projects will come in handy in your spare-time recreational pursuits, whether it be picnicking, hunting, fishing, shooting, camping, or boating.

As you pursue some or all of these projects, keep in mind that safety comes first. No project, large or small, is worth even a bruised thumb. Follow all common safety precautions. If you do not know how to use a power tool safely, or how to accomplish a certain procedure, we urge you to seek out qualified help before you start the work.

We also urge you to take double precautions when working with electricity. Whenever you plan to work on your electrical system, in most all cases it is best to shut the power off at the main power switch instead of just turning off the circuit you will be working on. Because of the way some homes are wired, the circuit can appear to be switched off, but still be hot. If you shut off the electrical power just with the circuit breaker, be sure to double-check the wires you will be working on with a tester before proceeding.

Many of our readers take an interest in do-it-yourself projects mainly to save money. There is no question that accumulating a basic set of tools and learning how to use them on projects around the home can save you big money over the years. But we also urge you to shop wisely when you can't do home improvement work yourself, or when you are buying major items like appliances or floor coverings. It doesn't pay to save money on smaller projects, just to waste it on some major purchases that turn out to be less than you expected.

A case in point. This past year we had a section of galvanized steel water supply pipe that began leaking. Because of other pressing work, we decided to hire a large plumbing firm to replace that section of pipe, which was about six feet long. A plumber from the firm arrived and produced an estimate of $795 to do the work—a head-shaking situation to say the least. However, a call to a different independent plumber the same day resulted in getting the pipe replaced within three hours for a total bill, including materials, of $97.

Some firms in the home repair business scour the world for the unwary. Try not to be one of them.

Gene L. Schnaser, Publisher

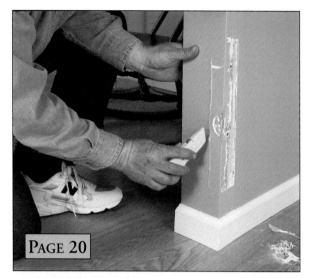

PAGE 20

PAGE 46

PAGE 64

CONTENTS

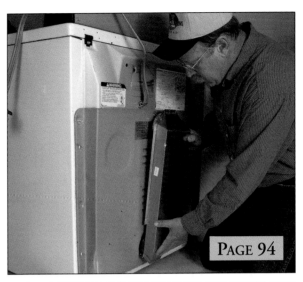

PAGE 94

PAGE 158

PAGE 168

ALL-TERRAIN CABIN

A VERSATILE OUTBUILDING THAT YOU CAN BUILD VIRTUALLY ANYWHERE TO GET YOUR SPECIAL PLACE

This eye-catching 16′ x 16′ building goes up fast and its simple, uncluttered design allows it to serve virtually any purpose you can imagine. It can be a wilderness cabin, a guest house, an office, a workshop, a studio, or even a fitness center.

Best of all, the structure can be built on almost any terrain, from the average backyard to the wild, rocky side of a mountain. In fact, the rougher the ground is where you build it, the better it seems to look.

The interior can be arranged in a variety of layouts to suit your needs. The version shown was made into a family health spa, complete with a sauna, a soaking tub, a full bathroom, and plenty of space for weights and exercise machines.

The framing can be finished with drywall or paneling. A loft could be built in the attic to gain additional space for storage or sleeping. (If you install a roof window, as in the version shown, the loft would provide a spectacular view on clear, starry nights.)

To cope with long, dark winters, this little building was designed to minimize heat loss while providing an abundance of natural light. Electric baseboard heaters were used for a heat source. Double-insulated low-E windows, a plywood-and-Styrofoam door, and plenty of insulation were used to keep the interior cozy.

FOUNDATION & FLOOR

Although this structure can be built on a traditional concrete perimeter or slab foundation, a much simpler

The cabin's skylight, centrally-located in the hip roof, spreads sunlight throughout the interior. Inside walls were finished with cedar paneling with matching moldings.

system was used for the version shown: reinforced concrete piers and Glulam beams.

This method elevates the building about 3′ above the ground and offers several advantages. It is easier than building a traditional foundation, it raises the structure above ground moisture and all but the tallest snowdrifts, and it makes it easy to keep out mice and insects, even in isolated areas.

The pier foundation can be built in half a day. If you have ever poured a perimeter or slab foundation, you will agree that's a big advantage. It took two persons less than two hours to install 12″-dia. waxed cardboard Sonotube pier forms, even though the site was rocky ground. A ready-mix concrete truck arrived an hour later, and the piers were completed before lunchtime. Post-base connectors were embedded in the tops of the piers before the concrete set.

After the concrete set up, the Glulam beams were laid on top of the piers, leveled with shims, and attached to post-base connectors with bolts. Then the floor joists were installed on 16″ centers.

To build the sealed floor, ½″ plywood was attached to the bottom of 2x6 floor joists, and the space between the joists was filled with R-21 fiberglass insulation. Next, ¾″ APA Sturd-I-Floor plywood was attached to the top of the joists. Since the goal was for the floor to have a thermal efficiency of at least R-30, 2″-thick (R-10) Styrofoam rigid insulation was added to the bottom of the floor.

Note: In this project no protective covering was added to the bottom of the Styrofoam. Some building codes may require a plywood or plastic covering over the foam insulation to keep out pests.

The walls were made of 2x6 studs and ½″-thick APA plywood sheathing. Although plywood is more expensive than waferboard or particleboard, it is stronger and more resistant to moisture. The 2x6 walls were insulated with R-21 fiberglass.

Windows can be installed almost anywhere in the building. In this project a large garden window was installed on the south side, and smaller windows were installed on the other sides and in the roof to lighten up the interior. Window sizes were used that would interrupt the structural framing as little as possible. All the windows had double-insulated low-E glazing.

Instead of installing the entry door in a wall, it was placed at an angle in a corner. This complicated the wall framing somewhat, but it didn't change the roof framing. Of course, you can place the door in a wall wherever it best suits your layout.

The finished cabin provides ample room for exercise equipment, as well a sauna, full-size bath, and a small soaking tub.

The exterior of the cabin's 6″-thick walls were finished with composite lap siding; the roof was fitted with steel roofing.

The foundation, of piers and beams, is fast and easy to build. The piers also give the cabin a unique appearance.

Piers were made with cardboard forms. Beams attached to them with post-base connectors embedded in the concrete.

HIP ROOF FRAMING

To simplify construction, the roof was made square. This made it easy to frame the top center for the Velux roof window. A hip roof is typically harder to build than a conventional gable roof, but it is not as difficult as it may look if you frame it one section at a time.

You may not be able to cut all of the pieces before you start framing, as a professional roof framer would do. However, the cutting process soon becomes obvious as you proceed, and you can do it by cutting and installing one piece at a time.

A hip roof distributes roof loads down and out, so tie beams are needed to hold the structure together and reinforce the walls. (Since the roof was built, it has stood up to more than 5′ of wet snow without consequence, so the design has proven strength.)

The four 2x6 tie beams were extended from wall to wall inside the building and were bolted to the top of the plate. They were laid flat to provide more overhead clearance inside the cabin. Using the tie beams as a nailing surface, a flat ceiling of ¼″ rustic-cedar paneling was installed. This approach simplified the overhead finish work.

The ceiling was insulated by stacking layers of fiberglass batts on top of the paneling instead of fitting the insulation into the roof framing and then paneling all of the roof angles. The opening for the roof window was boxed in and paneled to provide an unusual but effective source of interior light. On warm days, when the roof window and the other windows are opened, the updraft creates a cooling breeze.

INTERIOR COMPLETION

The walls and ceiling were finished with cedar paneling, with matching moldings made from cedar boards. The paneling was dark, but the light from the greenhouse window and roof window make the interior feel light and airy. The shower walls in the bathroom were paneled with epoxy-sealed red cedar. The epoxy coating waterproofed the cedar and created a smooth, shiny surface that looks good and is easy to clean.

In addition to a full bathroom, a Finnleo sauna was also installed. It is free-standing and could be placed anywhere in the building. The sauna was shipped as a kit with the heater, accessories, and complete installation instructions included.

An insulated box was built of ¾″ APA pressure-treated plywood to house the utility connections. The box was buried 4′ underground, and the interior was lined with 2″-thick Styrofoam. This weatherproofing system

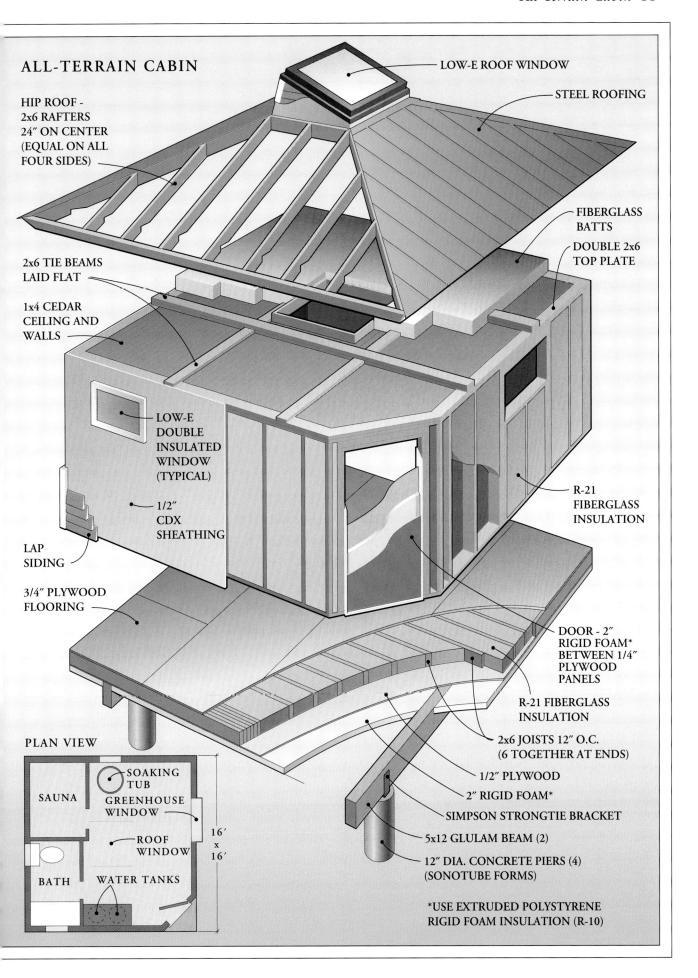

ALL-TERRAIN CABIN

LOW-E ROOF WINDOW

STEEL ROOFING

HIP ROOF -
2x6 RAFTERS
24" ON CENTER
(EQUAL ON ALL
FOUR SIDES)

FIBERGLASS
BATTS

DOUBLE 2x6
TOP PLATE

2x6 TIE BEAMS
LAID FLAT

1x4 CEDAR
CEILING AND
WALLS

LOW-E
DOUBLE
INSULATED
WINDOW
(TYPICAL)

1/2"
CDX
SHEATHING

R-21
FIBERGLASS
INSULATION

LAP
SIDING

3/4" PLYWOOD
FLOORING

DOOR - 2"
RIGID FOAM*
BETWEEN 1/4"
PLYWOOD
PANELS

R-21 FIBERGLASS
INSULATION

2x6 JOISTS 12" O.C.
(6 TOGETHER AT ENDS)

1/2" PLYWOOD

2" RIGID FOAM*

SIMPSON STRONGTIE BRACKET

5x12 GLULAM BEAM (2)

12" DIA. CONCRETE PIERS (4)
(SONOTUBE FORMS)

*USE EXTRUDED POLYSTYRENE
RIGID FOAM INSULATION (R-10)

PLAN VIEW

SAUNA

SOAKING
TUB
GREENHOUSE
WINDOW

ROOF
WINDOW

16'
x
16'

BATH

WATER TANKS

The south-facing Milgard garden window channels extra light into the interior, and the plants add a touch of color.

has also proven itself, with no water pipe freezing in sub-zero Montana winters.

All of the plumbing, including a 30-gal. pressurized storage tank, was located in a cedar cabinet. The panels are removable for easy access when maintenance is necessary. The top of this cabinet was sealed with epoxy to give it a tough, waterproof surface.

The entry door is a plywood-and-foam sandwich made with ¼″ rough-sawn exterior plywood panels glued to 2″ (R-10) Styrofoam with epoxy. A double-insulated low-E window was custom-made by a local glass shop to install in the door.

EXTERIOR FINISHING

The structure shown was built in the woods, where the danger of fire is relatively high, so steel roofing was used. Metal roofing is durable and can be installed as quickly as shake shingles.

The deck is 2x6 fir. A router with a ½″ rounding-over bit was used to round the edges of the fir. The round edges give the decking a cleaner finished look and make it safer for bare feet and easier to finish and maintain. The decking was attached to the joists with 3″ zinc-plated deck screws driven through clearance

After the floor was insulated and sealed, the 2x6 walls and the roof were put up and sheathed with ½″ APA plywood.

This view through the door shows the new sauna, plus the interior framing for the roof window and the 2x6 tie beams.

An angled entry door was installed at one corner of the cabin, though you could also take a more traditional approach.

holes. Each screw was countersunk slightly. The deck was finished with an oil-base preservative.

The exterior of the building was finished with composite lap siding nailed to studs with stainless-steel nails. Caulking was used on the siding seams and joints, as well as the joints around the doors and windows, and anywhere else a crack or gap was found.

The floor was given a non-skid surface similar to that found on boat decks. To finish the floor, first the wood was sealed with epoxy. When the epoxy had cured, the areas that wouldn't be painted were sealed off, then the paint was applied. While the paint was still wet, it was sprinkled with masonry sand. After a few days, the excess sand was vacuumed off and another coat of paint was applied.

Note: A spiral-bound construction booklet and blueprint outlining the construction process of the all-terrain cabin is available from the builder for $27 postpaid. The helpful information details hints, tips, and procedures, and is presented in sufficient detail so that either amateur or first-time builders can successfully erect the building. The booklet also contains material sources and optional floor plan layouts. To order, write The Butlers, P.O. Box 2010, Sandpoint, ID 83864.

The cedar entry step was screwed to the subfloor, caulked, and treated with wood preservative, like the deck boards.

The deck is of 2x6 fir lumber rounded with a router. The door is made of rough-sawn plywood glued to 2″ Styrofoam.

After taking a sauna, bathers can cool off with a quick shower in the cabin's full-sized bathroom, just a quick step away.

ALL-TERRAIN CABIN SOURCES

❑ **Baseboard heaters.** TPI Corp., Box 4973, Johnson City, TN 37602; (423) 477-4131.

❑ **Caulking and sealants.** Ohio Sealants, 7405 Production Drive, Mentor, OH 44060; 800-321-3578.

❑ **Composite lap siding.** Louisiana-Pacific Inc., 111 S. W. Fifth Ave., Portland, OR 97204; 800-547-6331.

❑ **Construction tools.** Angle-framing nailer, air compressor, power miter saw, tablesaw, and portable generator: Sears, Roebuck & Co.

❑ **Epoxy, fillers and accessories.** Gougeon Brothers Inc., Box 908, Bay City, MI 48707; (517) 684-7286.

❑ **Faucets and sinks.** Moen Inc., 25300 Al Moen Drive, N. Olmstead, OH 44070; 800-553-6636.

❑ **Fir decking.** Western Wood Products Association, Yeon Building, 522 S.W. Fifth Ave., Portland, OR 97204; (503) 224-3930.

❑ **Fiberglass insulation.** Certainteed, 750 Swedesford Road, Box 860, Valley Forge, PA 19482; 800-523-7844.

❑ **Glulam laminated wood structural beams.** Boise Cascade, Box 62, Boise, ID 83728; 800-237-4013.

❑ **Hydrotherapy soaking tub.** Snorkel Stove Co., 4216 Sixth Ave. S., Seattle, WA 98108; 800-962-6208.

❑ **Heavy-duty structural beam brackets.** Simpson Strong-Tie, 4637 Chabot Drive, Suite 200, Pleasanton, CA 94588; 800-999-5099.

❑ **Low-E vinyl windows.** Milgard Windows, Box 11368, Tacoma, WA 98411; 800-562-8444.

❑ **Paint.** Sherwin-Williams Co., 101 Prospect Ave. N.W., Cleveland, OH 44115; (216) 566-2000.

❑ **Plywood and panel products.** APA—The Engineering Wood Association, Box 11700, Tacoma, WA 98411; (206) 565-6600.

❑ **Roof window.** Velux-America Inc., Box 5001, Greenwood, SC 29648; 800-888-3589.

❑ **Rustic cedar paneling.** States Industries Inc., Box 7037, Eugene, OR 97401; (503) 688-7871.

❑ **Sauna Kit.** Finnleo, 575 E. Cokato St., Cokato, MN 55321; 800-346-6536.

❑ **Stainless-steel nails.** Manasquan Premium Fasteners, Box 669, Allenwood, NJ 08720; 800-542-1979.

❑ **Steel roofing.** Vic West Steel, East 6207 Desmet Ave., Spokane, WA 99212; 800-456-9124.

❑ **Styrofoam rigid polystyrene foam insulation.** Dow Chemical Co., Plastics Dept., Customer Information Center, Box 1206, Midland, MI 48674; 800-441-4369.

Cedar-scented heat from the sauna shown above provides a festive atmosphere. It's positioned next to the cabin bath.

This red cedar soaking tub found a home in the cabin, as well. Here it sits on blocks after receiving a coat of epoxy.

This cabin boot grate is constructed of two-tone, rot-resistant woods that will look good and will serve for many years.

CABIN ACCESSORY

This easy-to-make wood grate will look good in front of any cabin and, better yet, it will help keep the inside clean. Scuff your boots across the top of the grate; sand and mud will stay outside where it belongs.

Although the grate can be made of virtually any wood, rot-resistant species, such as redwood, cedar, and cypress are best. The grate here is redwood and cedar, two color-contrasting woods that will hold up for years. Tight knots and uneven grain are perfectly acceptable because they add character to the finished project. However, it is best to avoid wood with loose knots and splintery or separated grain.

To begin this project, first assemble the grate's perimeter framework. The frame is of 2x4 redwood with 3"-long No. 12 Phillips-head wood screws fastening the corners. Two screws are used in each of the corners, and the countersunk screw holes are sealed with ½"-diameter wood plugs.

The front and back 2x4 redwood pieces are 30" long and the two side pieces are 21" long. Lay the pieces on a flat, level surface and clamp the framework together while drilling screw holes. Use a square to make sure the framework fits properly.

After the perimeter framework is assembled, cut and install the two interior supports. The supports are ripped from a redwood 2x4, down to 1⅞" wide by

1½″ thick by 18″ long. The two supports are positioned flush with the top of the framework and then held in place at each end with a 3″-long No. 12 screw which is countersunk and plugged.

After the perimeter frame and the supports are completed, carefully hand plane the top of the framework so that all top surfaces are level and flush. Next, use a router to cut a ⅜″-wide, ½″-deep rabbet/notch around the top edges of each of the three compartments.

Use a sharp carbide router bit and go slow to prevent splintering the wood. With that done, turn the frame on its side and use a sabersaw to cut a 1″-wide slice of wood off the bottom edges, between the corners, to keep the frame from wobbling on a rough surface.

The top strips are western red cedar 1½″ wide and ¾″ thick. Select the wood's best side and place that side up. Cut and fit each strip individually and provide about ½″ of space between each strip. Using a rasp and sandpaper, fit the corners of the strips to the corner rounds left by the router bit.

The strips can be held in place with a wood glue rated for outdoor use, or you can use silicone. Silicone can provide a sufficiently strong bond and can also provide a degree of waterproofing to the ends of each strip. Silicone also eliminates the need for screws or nails and helps seal the rabbet.

Apply silicone in a generous bead all around the inside of the notch. Carefully lay the strips in place, gently forcing them down to the bottom of the notch with the proper gap between each strip. If needed, place small weights across the strips to hold them in place. Wipe the excess silicone seal off with a paper towel.

With the rabbet cut ½″ deep, the ¾″-thick scraping strips are left ¼″ high to provide a raised surface for removing debris from boots and shoes. If the soft wood wears down in spots from use, it can be re-leveled with a few passes from a sharp block plane.

After all the strips are set in place, leave the grate overnight to allow the silicone to cure. The grate can be left natural, it can be oiled slightly using boiled linseed oil, or it can be finished a number of other ways.

A 3½″ x 8″ piece of 3/16″-thick acrylic sheet can be cut out and screwed to the side of the grate for use as a boot scraper. The scraper could also be of iron or aluminum. But acrylic is tough, yet easy to cut using woodworking tools. After cutting, bevel the top edge with a block plane. Attach the scraper so it projects about 2″ above the edge of the grate. Drill the attachment holes slightly larger than the diameter of the attachment screw to prevent splitting the acrylic.

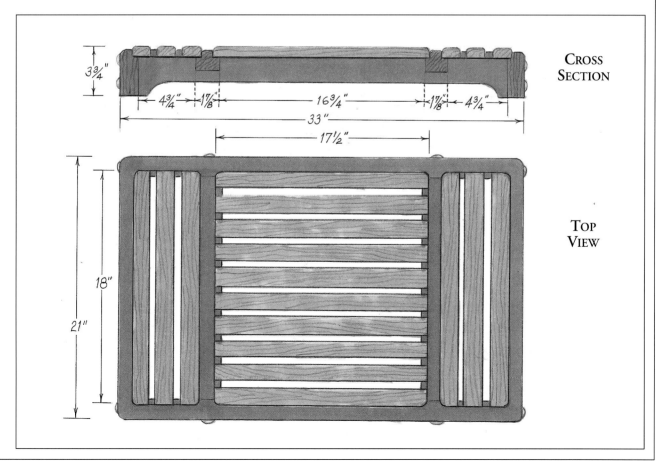

CROSS SECTION

TOP VIEW

WALL CORNER REPAIR

A MINI-COURSE ON HOW TO
REPAIR DINGS & DAMAGE
ON DRYWALL CORNERS

If you have ever smashed something heavy into the outside corner of a wall, you know the sinking feeling that follows. If the metal corner bead has been crushed out of shape, it is easy to see that no amount of spackling or wallpaper is going to disguise the unsightly damage.

Repairing damaged corner bead, however, is really not that difficult. With a few common tools, and less than $10 in supplies, you can make a seamless repair in a matter of hours. You may need to wait overnight for the first application of drywall compound to cure, but there is seldom more than an hour or two of work involved. It's a straight-forward repair.

The supplies needed to fix one or more damaged corners likely will cost you less than $10. These include a small tub of premixed drywall compound (mud), a length of metal corner bead, and a few fasteners, either nails or drywall screws. Expect a gallon of compound to cost around $6, and an 8′ length of bead about $2. This is much more material than you will need, of course, so you may want to shop around for smaller quantities. But if you have to go the full measure, the cost is small and you will have plenty on hand for the next wall repair.

ASSESSING THE DAMAGE

Corner bead dings come in all sizes. The smallest dings, those caused by a vacuum cleaner or a chair back, can usually be peened back into alignment. Just

Repairing damaged corners takes only a little time, some low-cost tools, and less than $10 in project supplies. Here the third, and final, coat of compound is being applied.

Begin by cutting out the finished compound along each side of the damaged bead to a width of 1½" to 2".

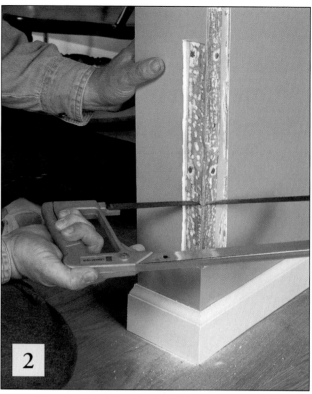

The compound will crack above and below the damage. Use a hacksaw to cut out at least 6" of the metal corner.

Use a pry bar to lift out the damaged section of metal. Pry firmly under the bead next to the nails, then pull the nails.

tap lightly with a hammer until the corner edge is reasonably straight, remove any loose compound, and apply vinyl spackling with a putty knife. Then, after the spackling has dried, you can sand lightly, apply another coat of spackling, and paint.

But for larger dings, where the metal bead has been crushed and bent out of shape, a more aggressive approach is required. It's difficult to straighten out metal after it really has been stretched. So the simplest approach is to cut out the damaged section—usually no more than 6″—and splice in a new piece of metal bead. While this may sound complicated, you will find that it is not.

WHERE TO BEGIN

Start out by cutting through the compound vertically, 1½″ to 2″ out from the corner on each side. A sharp utility knife works well here. In most cases you can expect some vertical cracks to extend above and below the point of impact. So be sure to make your cuts to include most of this damage as well.

With the perimeter of your repair established, use a screwdriver or a chisel to dig the compound away from the metal corner bead. Because you will be remudding this entire area, there is no need to be really careful. Just cut the perimeter and gouge out the center. Expect the old compound to pop out in pieces.

REPLACING DAMAGED METAL

With the metal bead exposed, use a hacksaw to cut across the bead about 3″ above and below the bent or damaged section. Then use a pry bar or a cat's paw tool to lift the damaged section away from the wall. The trick is to get under the nails that hold the bead in place, without prying against the remaining bead or the finished wall. If the nails are really stuck, and further prying seems likely to do real damage, cut the tin away from the nails with tin snips. Then countersink the old nails slightly with a hammer.

The repair piece you will splice in requires a tight fit, with the corners almost perfectly matched, so measuring closely is important. The easiest way to get a good fit is to hold a length of new bead against the old, over the missing section, and mark it with a pen or pencil. Then cut along this line with tin snips, cutting from each side toward the center of the corner.

You can use drywall nails or drywall screws to secure the new piece to the wall. Both work, but each has its

You can use a tin snips to cut off a section of corner bead. Cut from both sides, then bend it to break it into two pieces.

To determine length of repair piece, hold section of new bead against the old, corner-to-corner, and mark with a pen.

limitations. Nail heads lay flat against the bead metal, but the hammering will cause some vibration, which could cause more damage. Screws, on the other hand, are easy to drive in and cause no vibration. But their heads will protrude slightly, which can be a problem when mudding over them.

If the bead stands out fairly proud of the drywall, use screws. If not, you can use nails. If you use screws, you can drive them in with a power drill. Also consider adding screws to the existing bead, if needed, to further secure it. The important thing here is to make sure that the edges of the new metal bead match the old bead already in place. If, after securing the patch, you see that the edges are misaligned slightly, tap them very lightly with a hammer.

APPLYING COMPOUND

With the new metal patch in place, fill the void remaining with drywall compound. You will need two drywall knives, one 4″ to 6″ wide, and another 8″ wide. Using the narrower knife first, spread the compound over both sides of the bead.

Keep in mind that this first thick coating will shrink,

and that you will need at least three coats for a seamless finish. So don't invest a lot of time smoothing out the first coat and trying to get it perfect. Just lay it on, wipe it smooth and walk away.

After this first coat has cured—it usually takes several hours—use a hand sander to knock down the high spots and then spread a second coat over the first with the wider drywall knife. The goal with this second coat and all subsequent coats of compound is to apply a gradual, feathered sweep, both thinner and wider than the first coat. After this second coat dries in an hour or so, sand it lightly and then apply a third and final coat of drywall compound.

Again, make this final coating of compound both thinner and wider than the previous coat. It should be a paper-thin skim coat, meant only to fill tiny voids in the previous coatings of compound. If, after a final sanding, you still see imperfections, simply apply another skim coat.

Tip: It is always better to apply thin layers and have to add more than apply too much and have to sand more. When the repair appears seamless, sand very lightly, clean up the mess and apply two coats of paint.

6

Use screws or nails to secure the new piece of metal bead. If necessary, peen the edge lightly with a hammer to match up.

7

With patch in place, apply drywall compound to both sides. Then sand this first coat lightly after it has dried.

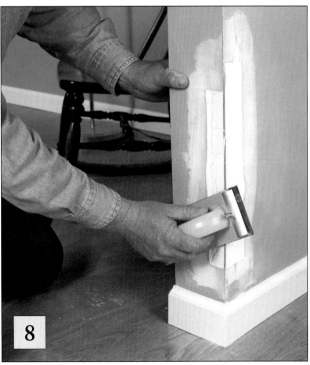

8

Apply a second coat with larger knife, allow to dry and sand. Apply third coat as shown on page 20, sand again.

SHELVING PROJECTS

HOW TO BUILD YOUR OWN SLOTTED SHELVING UNITS FOR USE AROUND THE HOME

If your home is typical, it is inundated with stacks of magazines, newsletters, mailers, catalogs, and every other kind of material that is hard to throw away. Not to mention all the other items around the home that need a place of their own.

The shelf design shown on the following pages will fill the bill in any home needing more shelf space. This unique room divider can be used anywhere around the home. It would work equally well in a sewing room, library, home office, or any place where lots of shelf storage would be handy.

Most of the tools and techniques used to build this unit will be similar to the ones you would use for any woodworking project. You can build this project with only three portable power tools—a sabersaw, a circular saw, and a power drill.

Add a router and you will greatly increase your efficiency. A tablesaw or radial-arm saw will, of course, help ensure square, true cuts. But if you don't want to invest in a major workshop saw, you can use a straight-edge-guided circular saw and invest more time and patience in setting up the cuts instead.

Even if you have a tablesaw or radial-arm saw, you will probably find it convenient to cut the plywood panels to rough size with a portable circular saw instead of trying to wrestle with full sheets. If you happen to have a bandsaw you will find it will come in handy for some operations which are a little easier than with a sabersaw.

Shelving projects of plywood, employing the slot technique, are within the do-ability range of even beginning wood-workers who only have small portable power tools.

This slotted shelf unit is relatively easy to build, and can be used inside or on a patio to display plants and store supplies.

Getting Started. Before you start, read the tips under Building Notes, page 32. This shelving unit is built of high-density overlay (HDO) plywood impervious to soil and water so it can even be used on a patio or in an attached greenhouse. It is free-standing and provides lots of storage area wherever you put it.

HDO plywood has a tough, smooth surface which is similar to plastic laminate and is easy to wipe clean. But, of course, you don't have to use HDO. Another tough, waterproof approach is to use painted medium density over (MDO) plywood. Or, you might want to select a hardwood plywood that fits your decor.

This project has a scalloped top and matching bottom cut-out design that suggests art deco styling. A pastel paint job would make it fit right in if art deco is the decorating theme in your home.

The shelves are cantilevered 8½″ past one side to provide a space for house plants that would be separate from other items, such as books and files. If this design doesn't suit your needs, you can make the unit symmetrical by changing the position of the slots in the shelves and making the partition wider. In any case, the shelves provide nearly 40 sq. ft. of space, enough for hundreds of books if need be.

The unit is 23⅞″ wide, and the shelves are 15⅞″ wide to allow for material lost to saw kerfs. The end result is heavy, strong, and stable, and makes efficient use of three sheets of plywood.

Cut Out The Parts. Cut the sides, shelves, and partition to their overall dimensions. Lay out the curves as shown and cut them with a sabersaw.

Tip: To cut the sides safely and accurately, begin by crosscutting a plywood panel to 72″. Then strike a line exactly down the center of the length of the panel. Cut down the middle of the line with a portable circular saw. Next, set your tablesaw fence for a 23⅞″ rip. With the factory edge against the fence, rip the two pieces to final dimensions.

Cut The Slots. Lay out the slots on one side and one shelf. Pay special attention when marking and cutting the slot locations in the shelves. Keep them square to the edge and the proper distance apart. If they are in-

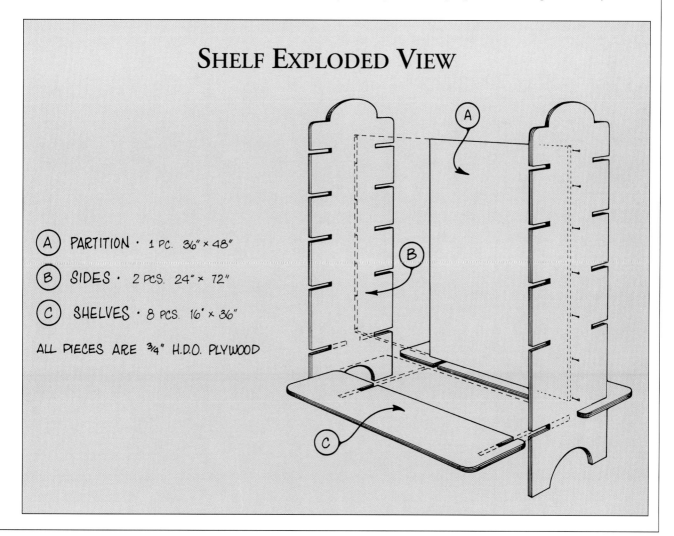

SHELF EXPLODED VIEW

(A) PARTITION · 1 PC. 36″ × 48″

(B) SIDES · 2 PCS. 24″ × 72″

(C) SHELVES · 8 PCS. 16″ × 36″

ALL PIECES ARE ¾″ H.D.O. PLYWOOD

SHELF PLAN DIMENSIONS

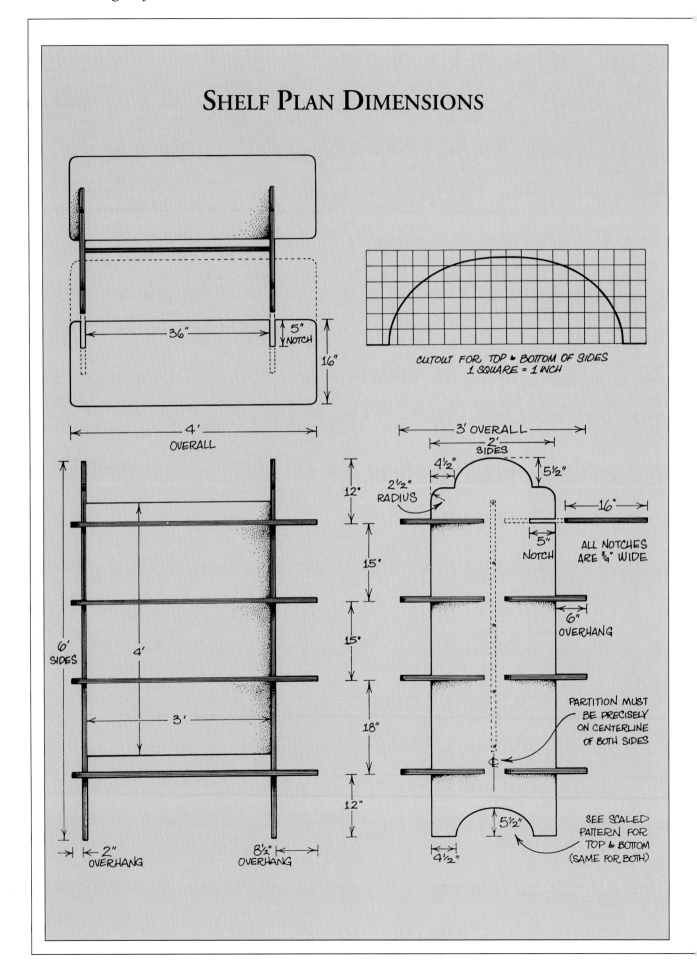

CUTOUT FOR TOP & BOTTOM OF SIDES
1 SQUARE = 1 INCH

36"
5" NOTCH
16"
4' OVERALL

3' OVERALL
2' SIDES
4½"
5½"
2½" RADIUS
16"
5" NOTCH
ALL NOTCHES ARE ¾" WIDE
6" OVERHANG
PARTITION MUST BE PRECISELY ON CENTERLINE OF BOTH SIDES
5½"
SEE SCALED PATTERN FOR TOP & BOTTOM (SAME FOR BOTH)
4½"

12"
15"
15"
18"
12"
6' SIDES
4'
3'
2" OVERHANG
8½" OVERHANG

accurate, the shelves will bind when installed.

If you force the shelving to fit one side because of a slight inaccuracy, it will affect the fit on the other side of the unit. Cut along the layout line with your saber-saw by cutting the line in two. Use a scrap of your shelf stock to check that the slots have proper clearance. The fit should be snug, but not so tight that you won't be able to assemble and disassemble the unit without pounding on it. If necessary, you can true up the cut with a file.

Now use the one side and one shelf as templates to rout the other side and shelves. Square the ends of the slots with the sabersaw after using the router. Check for fit. Then bevel each sharp edge slightly by making two or three passes with a block plane and a fine-toothed combination rasp, or you can use a ½″-wide file for tight corners.

Assemble The Sides. Fit the side to the partition with 2½″ #12 Phillips-head wood screws spaced 9″ apart. Begin by marking the exact vertical centerline on the inside of both side pieces. Drill ⅛″ holes through the centerline. These tiny holes will locate the pilot screw holes you will drill from the outside of the sides. To locate the partition during assembly, draw a vertical line exactly parallel and ⅜″ to one side of the centerline.

Because the parts are big and the unit isn't completely stable until the shelves are installed, you will need a helper for assembly. Have your helper hold the parts together while you drill pilots and countersinks and insert the screws. Wax the screw threads. To avoid stripping the wood, tighten them with a conventional screwdriver, not a power drill. This way you will be able to disassemble the unit for moving or storage.

Test-fit The Shelves. The shelves do not butt into the partition. A little space is left in case you want to run electrical wires, or to facilitate drainage if the unit is used in a greenhouse or outside.

Place the screwed-together unit upright on a flat, level surface and install both bottom shelves. Then work your way up, alternating sides to avoid racking the unit. If you prefer, you can leave a shelf out to

SHELF CUTTING LAYOUT

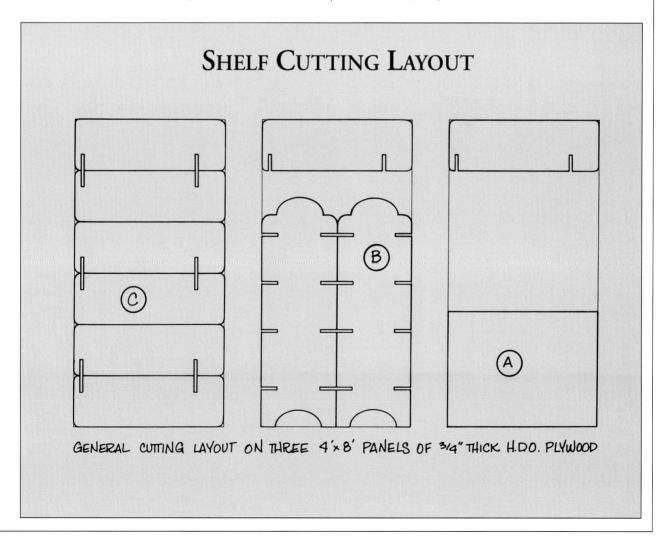

GENERAL CUTTING LAYOUT ON THREE 4′x 8′ PANELS OF ¾″ THICK H.D.O. PLYWOOD

make room for larger items.

Don't force anything. If a shelf binds as you insert it, use a file or rasp inside the slots to relieve the pressure. If the shelves end up slightly loose, wait until the finish is applied and then put a dab of silicone sealant into the loose slot and on the underside of the shelf where it won't be seen. When you disassemble the unit, you may have to break the seal by slipping a thin, flexible putty knife into the slot.

Apply The Finish. Disassemble the unit to make finishing easier. If you use HDO plywood, the only finish you need is two or three coats of Watco exterior oil applied to the edges. A disposable sponge brush works great for the job.

Apply a first coat and let it soak in overnight before applying a second coat. After a final coat, sand the edges smooth and flush with #80-grit sandpaper and wipe dry with a clean cotton rag. Use a mild soap to remove any oil from the HDO surface. You can apply furniture wax to the HDO if you want.

If you built your shelf unit from hardwood plywood, you can use an oil finish on the entire piece. If you built it from either soft or hardwood plywood, you can use varnish, polyurethane, or paint.

SHELF BUILDING NOTES

The techniques used to make this shelf unit can be mastered by beginners and can also be used for other designs. Following are some helpful tips to consider while building your project.

Cutting Slots. If you have only one or two slots to cut, the sabersaw is the tool for the job. You can mark out and cut a slot in just a few minutes. When there are several identical slots to cut, it will pay to set up a jig for a router.

However, you need to invest some time and care in making an accurate template for the slots, and you will still have to make the rough cuts with a sabersaw. A router equipped with a ½"-diameter flush-trimming or pattern bit will make a cleaner slot with more perfectly squared edges. You will need a rasp and file only to break the edges.

The flush-trimming and pattern bits used should be roller-bearing-guided straight bits. The flush-trimming bit, most often used to trim plastic laminate flush with the substrate, has the roller-bearing at the bottom of the bit. This works fine for template routing, except that the template must be on the bottom where you can't see it.

The pattern bit, designed specifically for working with templates, has the roller bearing on top. This makes it easier to use because you can keep your eye on the bearing surface. In addition, most pattern bits are designed to plunge. So if you have a plunge router you will be able to make closed slots without drilling a starter hole.

Make your template large enough so that you can clamp it to the workpiece without the clamps getting in the way of the router. Use a piece of high-quality ½"-thick plywood. Marine grade or multi-ply is ideal because there will be no voids. If you discover any voids in the laminates within the slot, fill them with wood putty. If the roller-bearing dips into a void it will ruin the slots. Hardboard, such as Masonite, makes an excellent template and doesn't have any voids. Sand away any saw marks.

Using A Router. To cut slots with a router, use the jig to draw your slots. Remove the jig and rout-cut the slots with a sabersaw. This may seem like extra work. However, remember that the router bit you are using is designed to trim material, not cut through it. You can make quick work of the sabersaw cuts by staying ¹⁄₁₆" to ⅛" within the layout lines.

Set the bit depth so the bearing rides on the template. Clamp or screw the template and workpiece to a stable surface. If it is an open slot, the open part should be facing you. Begin routing the slot at the right side, as the illustration on page 34 shows. Then rout around the back and the left side of the slot in one pass. This way the rotation of the bit works with you to hold the bearing firmly against the template.

When you are done routing, the corners of the slot will be rounded. In most cases you will need to square them with a sabersaw. If you will be making multiple slots in the sides of a cabinet to receive shelves, the set of slots in one side needs to be an exact mirror image of the set of slots in the other side.

Use your template to make all of the slots in one side. Then clamp the inside face of the routed piece to the inside face of the other side and use it as a template to rout the second set of slots. If there is any variation in the spacing of the slots in one side, it will be duplicated in the other side.

When you are done using your template, drill a hole

in one corner and hang it on a nail in your shop. You are bound to find a use for it again.

Using A Sabersaw. To lay out joinery slots that will be cut with a sabersaw, use a scrap of the material the slot will receive. Put the scrap in position on its edge. Lay out the cut lines by scoring with a sharp utility knife. Besides providing a very fine, accurate cut line, scoring the top veneer will prevent splintering.

If cutting a slot for a hand-hold or a wedge, it can be done by measurement because these slots don't have to be as accurate. Hand-holds are usually rounded on the ends and these curves can be laid out with a compass.

Sawing The Plywood. To protect face veneers, use a sharp hollow-ground, carbide-tipped blade. Cut with the good side facing up when using a tablesaw, radial-arm saw, or hand saw. The good side should be down when using a circular saw.

Even though a sabersaw cuts on the upstroke (and tends to splinter more at the top of the cut), sabersaw blades tend to wander slightly out of square. So it often is best to mark and cut with the good side up so that the most accurate cut will be on that side.

If you still have problems with splintering face veneers, there are a couple of tricks you can try. Lay a metal straightedge along your layout line and score it with a sharp utility knife. Press hard and make a few passes with the knife until you are completely through the face veneer. With the veneer fibers already severed they can't splinter when you saw.

Another method is to put masking tape along the area to be cut and then make your cut line on the masking tape. You can also put the masking tape on both sides of the cut. The tape will hold the veneer fibers in place as you cut.

Using A Circular Saw. To cut a large piece of plywood accurately and safely with a circular saw, the piece must be properly supported on both sides of the cut. When making crosscuts, one way to do this is by laying two 2x4s across two sawhorses and then laying the plywood on the 2x4s.

For ripping the length of the sheet, add a third 2x4 directly under the cut so both sides of the cut are supported. Set the depth of cut about ⅛″ deeper than the thickness of the plywood.

Another method is to use a sacrificial sheet on the ground and put your workpiece on top. Set your depth of cut so that it cuts through the workpiece and into the sacrificial piece. Then climb aboard and make your cut. This method works particularly well for thin, floppy plywood because it supports the entire sheet.

If you make final cuts with a circular saw, it is important to guide the saw with a straightedge, which can be just a straight piece of plywood or solid wood. This can be a bit time consuming. First align the blade to your layout line and make sure the saw base is square to the work. Then align the straightedge to the base and clamp it down.

You can speed the job and ensure accuracy by making a jig like the one shown below. This jig has a base of ¼″ plywood with a guide of ¾″ plywood screwed to one edge. Leave the base wide. After the jig is assembled, run the saw along the guide to trim the base to

STRAIGHT-EDGE GUIDE FOR CIRCULAR SAW

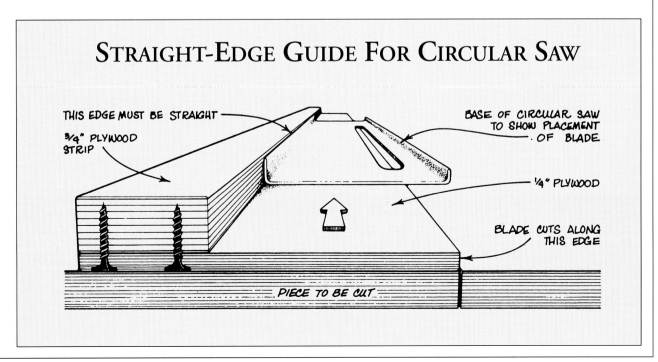

THIS EDGE MUST BE STRAIGHT

¾″ PLYWOOD STRIP

BASE OF CIRCULAR SAW TO SHOW PLACEMENT OF BLADE

¼″ PLYWOOD

BLADE CUTS ALONG THIS EDGE

PIECE TO BE CUT

width. Now you have a jig that is customized to your saw. All you need to do is align the edge to the cut line on the workpiece.

You can make the jig even easier to use by making a T on one end. Just screw another piece of ¾″ plywood to the bottom of the base, perpendicular to the guide. Now the jig will automatically align your workpiece for a right-angle cut. You can make the jig any length. A jig 5′ long will give you a good all-purpose length that will let you cut the width of a full sheet of plywood in one pass, or the length of a sheet in two overlapping passes.

Using Screws. If you are driving screws close to the edge in solid wood, or are driving into a narrow pieces, such as a cleat, it is best to first predrill to prevent the wood from splitting. You will often find that you want to predrill and countersink or counterbore so that the screw sets in a neat hole on the surface, instead of crushing into the veneer.

If you want the screw head to be flush with the surface, predrill with a countersink. If you want the screw below the surface so it can be covered with a plug or putty, predrill with a counterbore bit. There are several types of pilot bits that predrill and countersink or counterbore in one operation. One kind, Fuller tapered bits, come with adjustable countersink/counterbore collars as shown in the illustration on the opposite page. For a countersink, drill just to where to bottom of the collar stops getting wider. Go deeper for a counterbore.

As with most pilot bits that countersink and counterbore you need to use a bit and collar that are sized for the screw you are using. If the bit is too big, the screw may not hold. If it is too small, you may break the screw or split the wood, especially when you are driving into hardwood.

You can buy wood plugs in little cellophane wrappers at the hardware store, but they often have the end grain running lengthwise like a dowel. Then the plug is obvious because this end grain is stuck in face grain. It also makes it difficult to shave them flush with a chisel. The problem with these plugs gets worse if you stain the project because the end grain of the plugs absorbs more stain and gets darker.

A better way is to make your own plugs with a plug cutter. If you are plugging solid wood, save a scrap

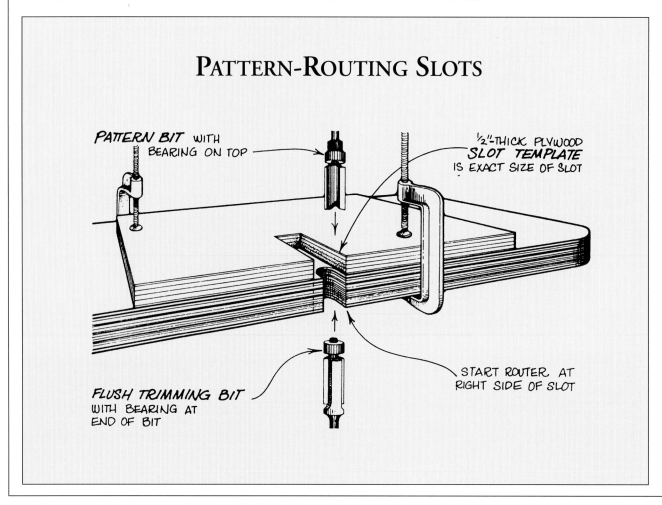

PATTERN-ROUTING SLOTS

PATTERN BIT WITH BEARING ON TOP

½″-THICK PLYWOOD SLOT TEMPLATE IS EXACT SIZE OF SLOT

FLUSH TRIMMING BIT WITH BEARING AT END OF BIT

START ROUTER AT RIGHT SIDE OF SLOT

DRILLING HOLES IN PLYWOOD

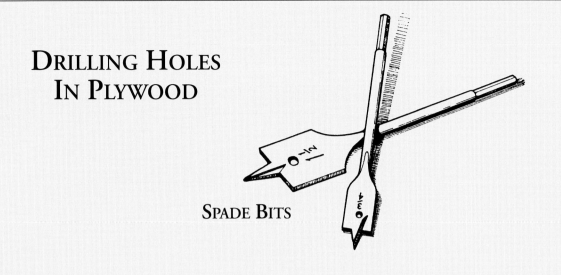

SPADE BITS

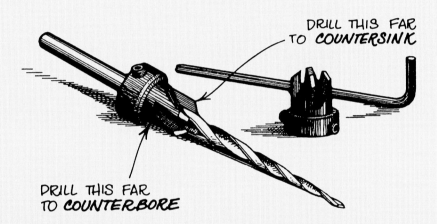

DRILL THIS FAR TO *COUNTERSINK*

DRILL THIS FAR TO *COUNTERBORE*

TAPERED BIT WITH COUNTERSINK & COUNTERBORE

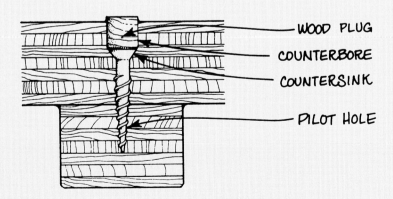

WOOD PLUG

COUNTERBORE

COUNTERSINK

PILOT HOLE

PROFILE OF PILOT HOLE, COUNTERSINK & COUNTERBORE

USING A FLEXIBLE LAYOUT BATTEN

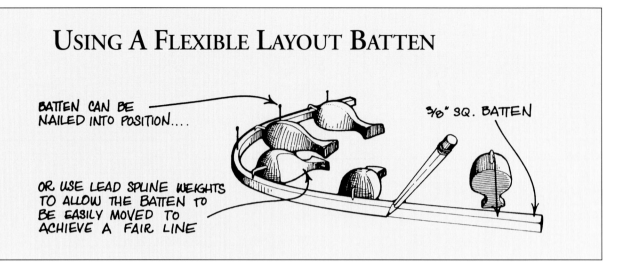

BATTEN CAN BE NAILED INTO POSITION....

OR USE LEAD SPLINE WEIGHTS TO ALLOW THE BATTEN TO BE EASILY MOVED TO ACHIEVE A FAIR LINE

⅜" SQ. BATTEN

from the project. If you are plugging plywood, use a scrap of the same species as the face veneer. Align the grain in the plug to the grain in the face. You can shave it flush with a chisel in seconds and you will hardly know the plug is there.

Dealing With Curves. To help lay out the curved portions of a project, use the grids if provided. Draw the grid with light pencil on the plywood, and then make reference marks on the squares. In some cases you will want to measure the squares provided where layout lines cross grid lines, and then use a scale ruler to transfer these measurements to the grid on plywood.

But usually curves are only decorative and you can just estimate the points. You may want to connect the points freehand. When measurements are provided from definite points, use a framing square and a tape measure to lay out the reference points. Again, you can connect the dots by drawing a freehand line if you trust your drawing ability.

Using A Layout Batten. Most people, however, find it difficult to freehand an unwavering, curved line. To help draw long, gradual curves you can use a thin strip of clear, straight-grained stock about ¼" wide by ¼" or ½" thick. Avoid knots and other irregularities which will distort the curve.

Determining the width of the rip is a matter of trial and error. The strip must be thin enough so that it doesn't have wows that will distort the curve. Start with the thickest rip you think might make the bend. Rip it thinner as needed until it is just flexible enough. If there is a hard spot in the strip that resists bending more than the rest of the strip, you can make a few passes along the hard spot with a hand plane until it assumes the correct shape. The same thing can be

done on the ends of the batten if they are too stiff.

Lay out the reference points on the stock. Then drive tacks into the reference points and flex the curve along them. (Boat builders use heavy lead weights called spline weights or ducks to hold the batten, but finish nails will work almost as well.)

Have a helper hold the batten in position while you draw the curve. Or you can tack nails into the stock on either side of the batten, as necessary, to hold it in position. The idea is to let the batten assume a fair curve without irregularities. Eyeball the batten from different positions, adjust as needed, and when it is finally just right, draw the curve with a pencil.

Sanding Plywood. One nice thing about high-quality plywood is that it doesn't need much sanding. If you plan to paint your project or coat it with epoxy, the only sanding the plywood may need is to remove saw marks from the exposed edges using #60-grit sandpaper. Then you can sand all surfaces with #80 grit and/or #100 grit for varnish or oil. For a nicely-polished oil finish, sand between coats with #400-grit or #600-grit wet-or-dry sandpaper. These very fine grits actually polish more than they sand.

When sanding plywood, follow the same cardinal rule as for solid wood—sand only with the grain. This is particularly important for hardwood plywood because you might sand through the thin face veneer before you get all the scratches out. An orbital palm sander and a hand sanding block are choice tools for sanding hardwood plywood face veneers. But for edges and other sanding jobs, you might find that sandpaper disks work well. They attach to circular foam pads chucked into a drill.

Repairing Voids. Even top-grade plywood will have

small voids in the interior plys, unless you buy marine or multi-ply. Inferior grades will have larger voids. If you tap over the panel, you can sometimes hear the void as a change in pitch. If you hear a large void, you may want to plan your cutting strategy so you don't cut through it and won't have to repair it.

Because of its structural properties, epoxy makes a top-rate filler for voids. You can thicken the epoxy with commercially available filler. Or you can use sanding dust as a filler, by adding dust from the same wood as the face veneer. In situations where strength is important, you can set the piece on edge and pour un-thickened epoxy into a void until it is filled.

If you aren't working with epoxy and you are filling just for appearance or to give a piloted router bit a smooth path, then any wood filler such as Plastic Wood will work fine.

Breaking The Edges. It is best to routinely cut a small chamfer or round on all unprotected plywood edges. Doing this makes the edges more appealing to the eye and the hand. It also protects the face veneers from chipping and provides a better surface for a finish. So also consider breaking edges that will not show. The only edges that are not candidates for breaking are those that are joined to another piece.

To create a slightly rounded edge, use sandpaper. For a chamfer, use a block plane or file. The block plane produces a smooth, finished chamfer on an edge that is parallel to the grain of the face veneer. But when used across the grain of the face veneer, it may splinter the veneer. So use a file for cross-grain chamfers.

Applying The Finish. Penetrating oils, such as Watco Danish Oil, tung oil, or boiled linseed oil, are often favorites for hardwood plywood that will be used indoors. Oil finishes provide a low-luster finish that shows off the grain of the wood. It is easy to apply and can be renewed by applying more oil. If an area gets damaged, you can sand and re-oil it.

You can apply oil finishes with a soft rag, especially the second and third coats that get rubbed in well. Keep in mind that heat can build up in oily rags and cause a fire. So make sure you keep the oily rags in water and dispose of them properly. You can use a foam brush, paint brush, or, for large areas, a roller.

When painting plywood, use a good interior primer and paint for inside projects, and exterior primer and paint for exterior projects. Both interior and exterior paints are available in an oil or latex base. The latex is easier to apply and clean up. But for wood surfaces that will get a lot of wear, such as shelves, a coat of oil-based primer followed by two coats of semigloss or glossy oil-based paint will be most durable.

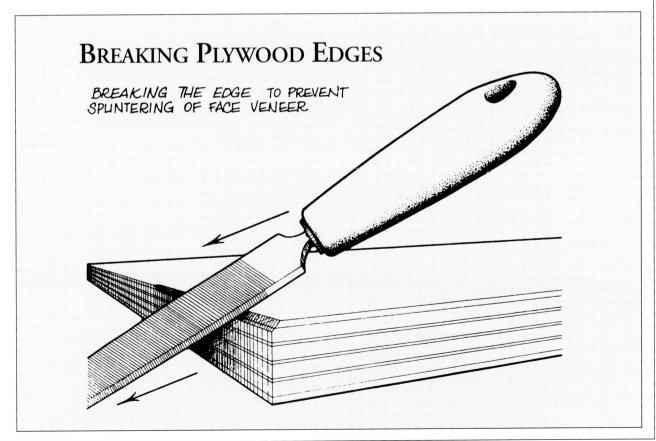

BREAKING PLYWOOD EDGES

BREAKING THE EDGE TO PREVENT SPLINTERING OF FACE VENEER

KITCHEN SINK UPGRADE

*MAKE LIFE IN THE KITCHEN
EASIER BY REPLACING A SINGLE-BOWL
WITH A DOUBLE-BOWL SINK*

If you are one of the millions of Americans who own a tract house, chances are good you may be saddled with a single-compartment kitchen sink. The very idea of affordable housing implies some cost cutting, and kitchens and baths have always offered the greatest savings potential to builders.

Which brings us to that modest, single-compartment sink. If it were simply a matter of removing it and installing a two-compartment model, you would probably have done so long ago. But a 22″ x 25″ sink often comes in a 27″ base cabinet, which simply won't abide a standard 22″ x 33″ sink. Until recently this situation would have left you with a make-do vs. major-remodeling decision.

Now, however, a few manufacturers offer 22″ x 25″ sinks that contain one standard-size compartment and one narrow compartment, which is ideally suited to be fitted with a garbage disposer.

The sink shown in this project is a Moen stainless-steel Camelot #22236 with a fourth deck hole. The fourth hole was used to support the control knob of a Geberit remote-control sink drain. This fitting allows you to drain the sink without plunging your hand into hot or dirty dish water. The faucet selected was a Peerless spray-spout #3608. The spout of this faucet can be used in the conventional fashion, or it can be pulled out on a hose for spray tasks.

And, finally, a ¾-hp Sinkmaster disposer was selected, primarily because it is so lightweight and easy to install. While disposers are commonly equipped for di-

Even a standard single kitchen sink can be upgraded to a versatile double sink without replacing the base cabinet.

Press plumber's putty around the underside of the sink's drain flange. Then insert the new drain through the sink hole.

rect wiring, this Peerless model was factory-wired with a conventional three-prong plug. In any case you need to bring 120-volt power into the base cabinet. Some codes may require you to provide a dedicated circuit and an under-sink disconnect.

PREPARING FOR INSTALLATION

To remove the old sink, shut off the water, either at the meter or inside the cabinet. Loosen the compression nuts and remove the sink trap. With this done, use a screwdriver to loosen the sink clips holding the sink to the bottom side of the countertop. Pull the sink from its opening and carefully scrape away all the plumber's putty left behind on the counter.

Because base cabinets are always cramped to work in, it makes sense for you to install as much equipment onto the new sink as possible before you finally set it in place. To protect both the new sink and the floor of the kitchen, do your work on top of a piece of cardboard or painter's drop cloth.

To install the drain/strainer in the new sink, begin by pressing a small roll of plumber's putty onto the bottom side of the drain's flange. Then press the drain into the sink opening. While most sink drains are secured by a spud nut tightened from below, the Geberit

To finish the drain installation, use a socket wrench to draw the two halves of the new drain strainer together.

If using a remote-control sink drain, attach the free end of the cable to the drain mechanism. It just snaps into place.

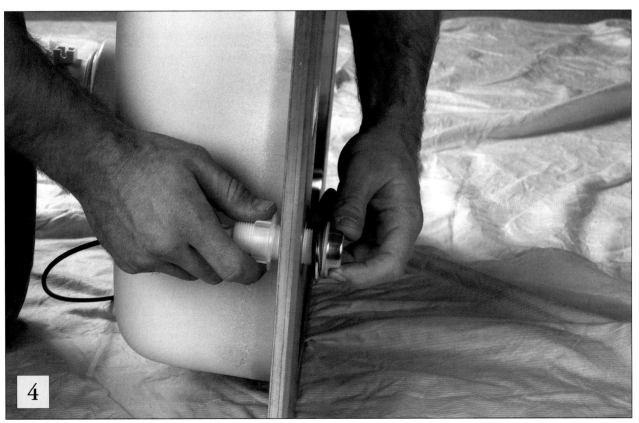

Mount the remote trip assembly in the fourth deck hole. Feed it through from below and tighten the nut from above.

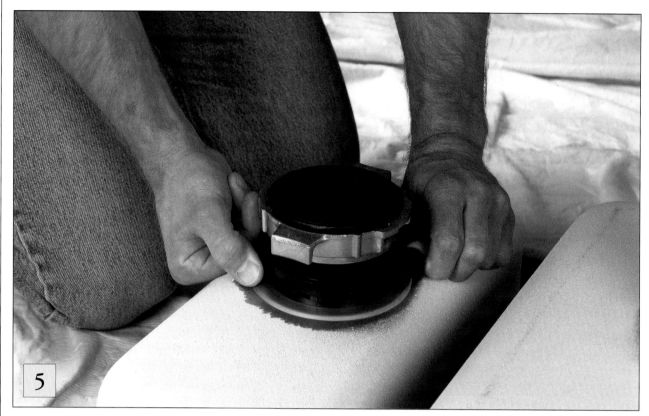

To fasten the disposer's drain spud in the sink opening, feed it through from above and tighten the large nut from below.

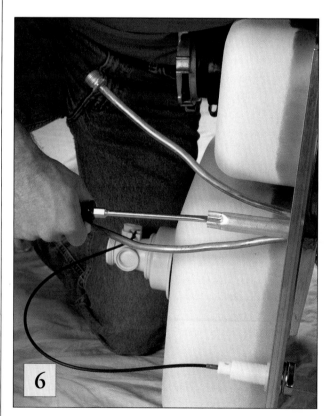

Feed the faucet supplies and shank through the sink's deck holes and tighten up the jamb nut using a deep socket.

drain uses a hollow hex-head nut to draw the upper and lower halves together. Use a socket wrench to tighten this bolt.

At this point, if you are using a drain similar to the Geberit, mount the remote-control knob in the fourth sink hole and connect the cable to the drain. Simply feed the unit's cable and fitting through the deck hole and then tighten the jamb nut.

INSTALLING DISPOSER & FAUCET

Installing the disposer drain assembly is also quick and easy. The disposer selected for this project used a simple plastic spud nut and neoprene sink gasket for installation. No putty was needed.

The gasket was simply placed on the drain flange and the threaded drain spud was inserted through the sink opening. Then the spud nut was tightened, with the locking ring and disposer gasket pressed onto the bottom of the spud.

Next, to install the new faucet, its supply tubes and its threaded shank were fed through the deck holes of the new sink. Then a bracket was slid over the threaded shank and the jamb nut was tightened against the bracket. To connect the spray spout, the hose was fed through the top of the faucet and threaded onto the

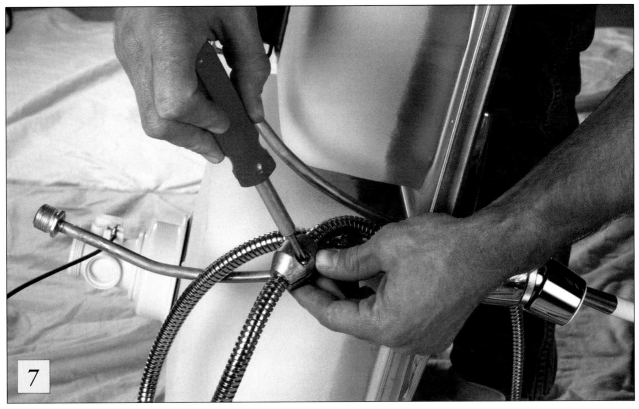

Screw the two halves of the stop nut over the sink hose to keep the hose from kinking whenever it is pulled too far out.

shank, using a light coating of pipe joint compound as lubricant.

SETTING THE SINK

With the faucet and drains installed, set the sink in the counter opening. Don't bother to use caulk or putty under the rim at this point. Instead, concentrate on securing the dozen or so sink clips provided. Each clip can be slid into the sink's support channels from the ends. Place one clip roughly every 6″. Then use a slotted screwdriver on the clip bolts to draw the sink down flush with the counter.

After the sink has been secured, lift the garbage disposer body up to its drain fitting and engage the locking ring. Then twist the locking ring until it reaches the stop tabs on the disposer.

To make the drain connection in this project, a plastic sink-waste kit was used. The first step is to join the drain/strainer and disposer. Start by connecting a flanged tailpiece to the sink drain, then extend a waste tee from the tailpiece. Install the waste ell on the disposer discharge pipe and connect the two sides of the sink with a 90° waste arm. Connect this assembly to a plastic P-trap and the P-trap to the permanent drain piping in the wall.

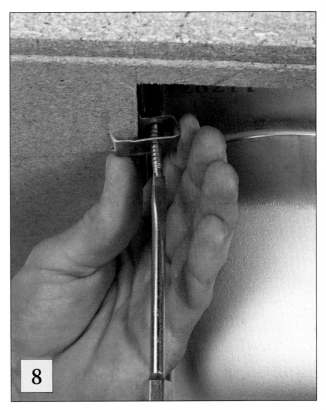

To tighten the sink against the countertop, use the sink clips provided. Slide clips into sink channel and tighten.

Lift disposer up to its drain assembly and engage its locking ring. Twist ring until it meets the stop tabs on the disposer.

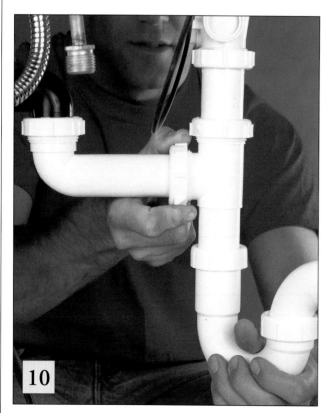

Use a PVC sink waste kit to join both of the drains to a plastic P-trap. The fittings need only be hand tightened.

With the disposer in and drain connections made, connect the water lines. The Peerless faucet used in this project had supply tubes with threaded compression fittings soldered on. This being the case, it was easier to use ball-head chrome supply risers. With this type of supply, the faucet nut and fitting compress the ball for a leak-proof joint. Be sure, however, to back-hold the compression fitting when tightening the nut.

To connect the supply tubes to the shut-off valves under the new sink, retrieve the ⅜″ compression nuts from the old risers and use new compression rings. Slide a nut and ring onto each of the supply tubes and then insert the tubes into the upper ports of the valves. Using a drop of liquid dish soap as a lubricant, tighten the compression nuts finger-tight, then add two full rounds with a wrench.

CAULKING THE SINK RIM

The best material for sealing the rim of the sink is latex tub-and-tile caulk. It has great adhesive qualities and is remarkably forgiving. Just wet the area around the rim and apply a bead of caulk. Then work it into the joint using your fingers. Finally, wipe away all excess with a wet rag. When the caulk dries, it will shrink slightly, leaving a nearly invisible seal under the rim.

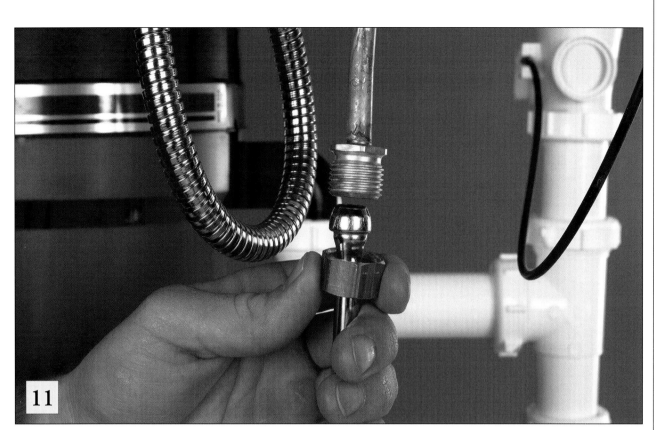

Use copper/chrome supply risers to connect water piping to faucet. The ball is compressed between the nut and fitting.

Connect the circuit ground to the switch and metal box. The disposer installed came wired with a three-prong plug.

A latex tub-and-tile caulk can be used to seal around the sink rim. After working it in, wipe away the excess caulk.

This handsome kennel house is easy to move about, it's well ventilated, plus the top opens up to a handy storage cubby.

K-9 Projects

A Pair of Projects That Will Make Your Best Buddy More Comfortable

Your dog deserves the best. The first project shown here, a sturdy but portable house, is perfect for trips to the field or as a more-permanent outdoor shelter. The second, a padded bed, gives your dog a comfy place to sleep other than cold, hard places.

KENNEL HOUSE

This kennel house is designed to be convenient while traveling for hunting, training or field trials, or at home under a tree in your yard. It is small enough to load into the back of a pickup or other sport utility vehicle, yet large enough to provide comfortable, year-around quarters.

The handles on each side of the house provide a method for easy lifting. The roof is hinged and allows quick access to a compartment for bowls, food, leashes, brushes, retrieving dummies, and other equipment. The size suggested is suitable for medium-size dogs weighing up to about 50 lbs., and the basic design can be adjusted as needed.

Optional aluminum-angle legs can be used to support the house above the ground, allowing air to circulate freely in hot weather. During cold weather the supports can hold the house above mud or melting snow to keep the bottom dry.

Aluminum angle is lightweight, easy to drill for screws or bolts, and doesn't rust. Two self-tapping screws per leg can be inserted through the 2″-wide aluminum angle and into the corner of the house for support. This independent four-corner suspension system can be adjusted to allow the house to sit evenly on sloping ground. Each leg can have a small foot pad of plywood epoxied onto the bottom to prevent sinking into mud or snow. The legs can be removed before placing the kennel in the back of a vehicle.

The house can be built in a hot-weather or cold-weather version, or a combination. The warm-weather

The house provides an independent four-corner suspension system that lets it set in a level position on any terrain.

For cold weather, 1″-thick sheet foam can be applied on the interior of the kennel house using panel adhesive.

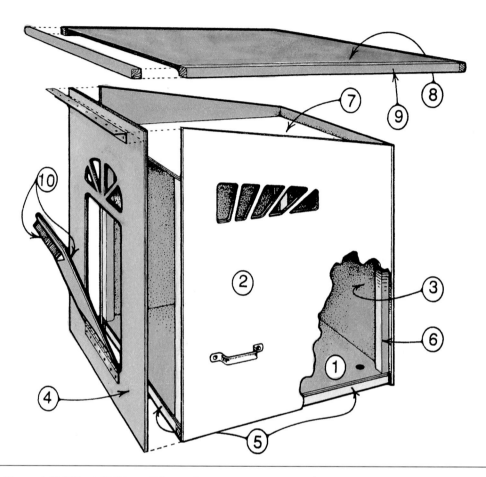

KEY: 1. Floor, 26″ W x 26″ H. 2. Sides, 26″ W x 33″ H. 3. Back, 26¾″ W x 27″ H. 4. Front, 26″ W x 33″ H (14″ x 16″ door). 5. Cleats, ¾″ square, cut to fit. 6. Corner Posts, 1⅜″ square x 25½″ L. 7. Bottom, 26″ W x 26″ H. 8. Roof, 30″ W x 30″ H. 9. Drip Rails, 1″ square, cut to fit. 10. Door Trim, cut to fit for handle and for gangway cleats on inside of door.

version should have numerous slots and openings, as shown, to promote ventilation. For cold weather, fitted pieces of 1″-thick sheet foam can be applied on the inside of the house, using panel adhesive to hold the pieces temporarily in place. For added comfort a removable dog bed made of heavy washable fabric and filled with aromatic cedar chips to repel fleas, can be placed inside the house.

The entire house can be assembled using APA marine grade ⅜″ plywood. A lightweight version could be made using ¼″ plywood, and a heavy-duty version can be made with ½″ plywood. The house is held together with 1″ screws and waterproof glue. The plywood floor should be sealed all the way around with caulk or epoxy. To aid with cleaning, you can cut drain holes in each corner so that the interior of the house will be easy to flush out with a hose.

This project is easy to build to any dimension by starting with the plywood floor. Once the floor size is determined, it is a simple matter to build around it by cutting each piece to fit. Attach the sides first, then the front and back pieces. The bottom and the overhead compartment floor are ⅜″-thick, with support cleats glued and screwed under the bottom of each. The corner posts are 1⅜″ x 1⅜″ clear fir. First cut and install all of the four corner posts to the height desired, then drop in the compartment floor, which is supported by the four corner posts.

To prevent snow and rain from getting inside the unit, attach a roof overhang. The overhang moldings should be 1″ x 1″ fir, which should be glued in place and sanded round on the edges. Use a wider overhang around the roof if rainfall in your area is high.

After the house is assembled, mark and cut the location of the door and optional vent slots. One good choice for the door and vent holes is shown in the drawing. Cut out designs with a fine-blade sabersaw, finish with a rasp, round file, and sandpaper. Attach hardwood cleats to the inside of the front door for traction. Also attach a cleat onto the outside of the door for a handle and door support. A quality enamel paint will protect the plywood for years.

Most hardware stores can provide piano hinges for the roof and door, as well as various types of door latches. The roof should also be latched if you plan to haul the unit in the back of an open pickup. Finally, attach two heavy-duty lifting handles onto each side of the kennel using bolts or machine screws.

CANINE COT

All dogs enjoy having their own bed and a warm place to sleep. A dry bed elevated off the ground keeps them healthier and cleaner, and less susceptible to pests and diseases. This project provides all these advantages.

The size is just about right for a medium-size dog, up to 40 or 50 lbs. However, the bed frame and mattress shown can be used as starter dimensions and adapted for other dog sizes and shapes. Add a pillow stuffed with cedar chips, and the bed is comfortable, smells fresh, and also helps repel ticks and bugs.

The bed is ideal for traveling and may be placed in a camper or the back of a pickup or mini-van for comfortable quarters on long trips. It also tucks in an out-of-the-way location, such as near a wood stove or on the shady side of the house in hot weather.

The bed has a hand-hold on each side and is easily portable for cleaning or a change of location. Your dog will appreciate having the bed positioned so that it will

This canine cot can be built to any dimension by determining the size floor you wish to have, then building around it.

The mattress of this canine cot can be of any durable material. It's elevated to be warm in the winter, cool in summer.

provide a good view of the activity around the house, but is not too far from the food bowl.

The framework is of ½"-thick APA marine plywood, which works well for projects that are exposed to extremes of moisture, wear, and weather. The framework holds the bottom of the pillow off the ground a few inches for ventilation. This helps keeps the bed dry in wet weather, and cooler in hot weather.

The frame is held together with screws and glue. The only hardware required are 1¼" No. 8 wood screws, which are inserted into the frame's bottom support cleats and into the plywood edges. Traditional cabinet glue will also work if the bed is kept relatively dry. Another good choice is epoxy glue. Small amounts of epoxy, along with instructional literature, can be ordered from Gougeon Brothers Inc., 100 Patterson Ave., Bay City, MI 48706; (517) 684-7286.

The first step in assembly is to measure and draw the bed-frame patterns full size on the plywood, and cut out the pieces using a sabersaw with a fresh, sharp blade. Clamp the pieces together on a flat, level workbench surface, and assemble the sides to the front and back using glue and screws.

Countersink for each screw as necessary, using the proper-size bit to prevent splitting out the plywood. If there is a problem with stripping threads, tighten the screws carefully by hand. Attach the support cleats to the inside edges of the sides, front, and back of the bed using glue and screws. Place the screws 4" to 6" apart and smear each cleat with glue before installing it.

Next, place the plywood bottom of the bed on top of the support cleats. Too tight of a fit may force the sides apart. If this is the case, trim the edges of the bottom panel. The bottom can be glued and also held in place with screws inserted down through the bottom panel and then into the support cleats. When the frame is assembled, sand all saw cuts and round all sharp edges with #60-grit sandpaper. Carefully remove all splinters. The final finish for the bed can be oil, paint, varnish, polyurethane, or it can be left natural.

Use a spade bit to drill a series of ¾" ventilation and drain holes in the bottom for hot or wet weather, or if the bed is left outside for a long time. Place the bottom of the bed over a scrap piece of wood while drilling to prevent splintering the backside as the drill exits. Drill at least one drain hole near each corner.

Any durable fabric can work to cover the mattress. The mattress shown is of tough, breathable Supplex fabric. Velcro fastening allows the cover to be removed and washed as needed. Supplex is available at most fabric stores, and can be stitched with a standard sewing machine and heavy thread. The mattress can be filled with foam padding, foam peanuts, cedar chips, or a combination of these materials.

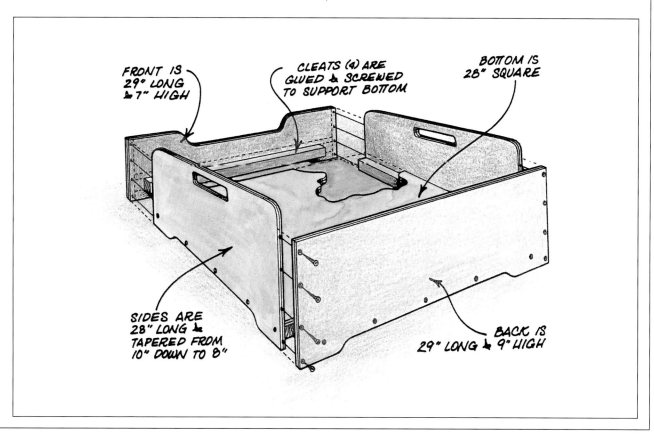

GLUING TECHNIQUES

TIPS ON SELECTING & USING
WOOD GLUES FOR
HOME WORKSHOP PROJECTS

If you are a do-it-yourselfer who builds projects in your home workshop, it will pay you to learn more about gluing. Good gluing techniques can actually mean the difference between a well-built project that lasts for decades, or one that can disintegrate quickly.

The process of gluing can be deceiving because on the surface it appears to be so simple. Theories abound on the best way to glue up wood, and most professional woodworkers develop their own methods. And so can you; the important thing is that they work.

SELECTING A GLUE

Most workshop projects of wood are assembled using aliphatic resins (yellow glues), polyvinyl acetates (white glues), and liquid hide glues. Other options for the do-it-yourselfer include two-part resorcinol glue and epoxies, plus newer polyurethane glues.

Resorcinol glue is a two-part glue that needs to be mixed. It is waterproof and not affected by heat or steam, making it good for exterior or marine projects. It produces brown or maroon glue lines and needs a clamping time of six to eight hours. Epoxies also need mixing and are extremely water resistant. But they do require some practice to use and, like resorcinols, require safety gear when using. The new polyurethane glues cure by being exposed to moisture, and are also worth considering if moisture resistance is important.

The yellow and white glues, however, are the most commonly used adhesives in working with wood. Of these two types, yellow glues are the most popular. While neither yellow or white glues are waterproof,

Although gluing up wood seems simple, selecting the right glue and using certain procedures can boost your success.

Applying just the right amount of glue provides enough to make a strong joint without having excess glue squeeze-out.

yellow glue is more water resistant and stronger than white glue. Both glues will usually set up within about one hour and cure to full strength in about 24 hours.

Glues work either by drying, cooling, chemical reaction, or a combination of these methods. Yellow and white glues work by drying; that is, by losing water from the glue line. After the glue is spread, parts are clamped together until the glue sets. During this time, the glue and water mix penetrates the pores of the wood. As the water goes through the pores, glue is retained on the wood fiber walls. The glue gains strength as the water leaves this adhesive film.

For furniture, most professionals use the original yellow aliphatic carpenter's glue because of its faster set-up and superior strength compared to white polyvinyl glue. The yellow glues won't produce as much "slippage" of parts during assembly as common white glues, and also won't clog sandpaper as much during finishing. You may want to use a common white glue formulation, however, if you need a longer time to set up parts before the glue sets.

You will find two types of yellow glues available, the original and a weather-resistant version which is formulated for projects that will see service outdoors, such as outdoor furniture, picnic tables, shutters, planters, mail boxes, or bird feeders. The weather-resistant version is also an aliphatic resin glue, but catalyzed; it's like a two-part glue already mixed together.

Both types of yellow glues resist solvents, heat, and water. The more weather-resistant yellow glue costs only slightly more than the original. If you are using it for the first time, be aware that it will set up faster than the original yellow glue. Though it is water resistant, it is not for projects that will remain below the water line, or will be continually submersed. It is, however, FDA-approved for use in cutting boards.

BUYING GLUES

If you have a particularly elaborate set-up, you may want to consider using a liquid hide glue. This glue will give you about three times the "open" time as the yellow aliphatic glues. Liquid hide glue is an old stand-by which is still being sold for use in antique repair and for building musical instruments. Purists like it for antiques because it often is the same kind of glue that was used originally. Instrument builders like it because it is a "reversible glue," meaning that by applying water to the joints, the glue will soften to allow adjustment of the parts for tuning purposes.

You can save big money if you buy glue in larger

If you have much gluing to do, you can save 75% or more by buying a gallon and transferring it to smaller glue bottles.

Inexpensive acid brushes, sold in soldering supply departments, do excellent work of distributing glue on narrow boards.

For wider areas, use an inexpensive nylon or china-bristle brush. Before using brush, clip off about half the bristles.

To spread glue faster on wide, flat areas you can use a 4"-wide paint roller. Select a roller with a short-length nap.

containers and pour it into smaller containers, either small plastic squeeze bottles or a plastic Tupperware-style glue pot. For example, while 8 ounces of yellow glue in a small plastic squeeze bottle might cost about $3.20, a full gallon of the same glue (the equivalent of 16 of those small 8-ounce bottles) might cost about $13.50, or only about 84 cents per 8 ounces.

When storing glue in other containers, be aware that coffee cans are a common source of iron contamination that can cause black glue lines. Glues with a pH of less than 7 will absorb iron from steel, and this dissolved iron will then react with certain woods, such as oak, walnut, mahogany, cherry, and other colored woods, to form a black glue line. Though this is less likely to happen with yellow glues than with white glues, it is still a good idea to avoid metal containers.

TOOLS FOR GLUING

The tools needed to do an adequate job of gluing don't need to cost much. Besides the glue you plan to use, you need a way to spread the glue after it is applied. A small 4″ paint roller can work well on larger, flat areas. For smaller areas a couple of inexpensive brushes will do the job nicely. Other gluing tools to consider include a couple of very sharp paint scrapers, a cabinet scraper, and a sharp wood chisel that is ½″ wide.

The brushes will help you apply the glue to the joints; the scrapers and chisel will help you get rid of the excess glue where it is not wanted. Paint scrapers with wood handles are preferred by some professionals because they don't flex as much as those with newer-style plastic handles. Those with carbide blades can work well, as long as they aren't used around screws or nails that can chip the blade. Paint scrapers with U-shaped blades offer more blade surface to use up through repeated sharpenings.

For spreading glue, one type of brush can be a throw-away nylon-bristled brush for wider areas that will cost you less than $2. The other type can be a smaller, inexpensive brush (usually called an "acid brush") for narrow or thin pieces that will cost you less than 25 cents apiece. Both types are available at hardware stores or home centers.

Select a nylon or china-bristle brush that is about 1½″ or 2″ wide. Before you put a regular paint brush to use for gluing, clip off a little more than half of its bristles. Doing this will make sure that the remaining bristles are adequately stiff so they won't slop glue around when you are using it on either the edges of boards or on mitered joints. Just remember to turn this

To store glue between jobs you can make up your own "glue pot" using two common plastic-ware containers.

To store gluing brushes in water, you can make your own container out of a recycled kitchen or bath product bottle.

wider brush edge-wise when using it to spread glue.

The acid brush is about ½" wide, making it handy for spreading glue on small or tight areas. It is sold for putting flux on metal before soldering, so look for it in the section of the store where soldering supplies are sold. To keep both the large and small brushes workable between projects, you can keep them immersed in plain water in a small recycled plastic container. The original container can be one that once held kitchen or bath products. Or use plastic-ware containers.

GLUING PREPARATIONS

Before beginning to glue up wood, consider the condition of the parts to be glued. If at all possible, start your project with cleanly cut, perfectly straight boards. Take any bow out of the boards before gluing by first face-jointing them and then planing them. By using straight and true boards you won't have to get into tricky clamping set-ups, and you won't have to force the boards in one direction or another while gluing.

When processing project wood, consider keeping the wood's dimensions slightly oversize before doing the gluing. Usually you will need to do additional processing of the wood after gluing anyway, so you might as well do it after the gluing rather than before. Also try to use sharp blades and bits. If dull tools are used, they can loosen (but not remove) a layer of fibers on the surface of the edges to be joined. When this happens the glue may not penetrate through this debris to solid wood, resulting in weak joints. A signal that this may be a problem is if any joints that have ruptured are coated with wood fibers.

Also try to make sure that each board you plan to glue has relatively the same moisture content. If, for example, one board has 15% moisture, while the boards next to it are at 8%, you can be asking for an irregular final surface. If you glue and plane boards with unequal moisture content, those with higher moisture will shrink more than the others. This can leave an irregular surface at the juncture of the glue line.

THE GLUING PROCESS

Once you have your gluing tools and project parts at hand, you are ready to start the gluing process. The goal is to have clean and dry surfaces, and to have parts fit together snugly. Also, on larger projects, try to first glue up subassemblies of small components to reduce the total gluing job into smaller steps.

Before you get started, be aware that glue will soak more into the end grain, and potentially result in starved glue joints. To help prevent this, you can "size" the end grain with a mixture of glue diluted with water. Dilute just enough so that when it is applied, glue drops don't form at the lower edges of the wood. Another method, somewhat less effective, is to coat the end grain with full-strength glue, allow it to dry 5 to 10 minutes, then re-coat with glue and assemble.

If you haven't had much experience with gluing, take the time to practice first with pieces of scrap wood. To edge-glue boards together, for example, first run a bead of glue across the edges to be joined, keeping the bead about ⅛" to ¼" wide. A good rule of thumb for any gluing is that a thin glue line and tight-fitting pieces will produce the strongest and least noticeable joints. Use the clipped nylon-bristle brush edge-wise to smooth out the glue, spreading it evenly across both board edges to be joined.

Once this is done, some woodworkers will pick up both boards and press the two edges together. While holding the boards together, the edges are rubbed back and forth a few inches a couple of times. This will further help to spread the glue on both edges so that each edge is evenly covered with a uniform layer of film. The next step is to clamp and allow the glue to dry.

The purpose of clamps is to bring pieces being glued into solid contact to produce a thin, uniform glue line and to hold the assembly together until the glue is strong enough to do the job. If the pieces fit together perfectly you wouldn't even need clamps. But since processing wood with home workshop tools is never exactly perfect, a certain amount of clamp pressure must be used. Applying pressure uniformly is actually more important than the amount of pressure used.

You won't need much clamping pressure if the edges of the wood parts are straight, true, and square. If you are gluing wood cut to exact dimensions, you may want to use clamp pads on the clamp jaws. Many professional woodworkers, however, seldom use clamp pads because they work with more precisely-cut wood and also know how to apply just enough pressure without overdoing it. (Note that if you glue up pieces that are oversize, you won't have to worry about using clamp pads or waste time trying to protect wood that is already processed to final dimensions.)

When clamping wood parts, you can use dowels between the wood and bar clamp jaws to help keep the pressure centered. Also, if you are gluing veneer to a wood surface, here's a procedure that can help you get good results: First use a sponge to wet the face of the veneer so that it won't curl. Then apply a thin film of

To reduce the prep and adjustment time per glue-up, divide larger projects down into smaller subassemblies, if possible.

A dowel between the jaw of a bar clamp and the wood to be glued helps to center the pressure and keep it uniform.

Use only as much clamp pressure as needed, check parts for squareness, and remove clamps shortly after the glue sets.

glue to both the surface and the underside of the veneer. Then, when the veneer is dry to the touch, you can use an old clothes iron at a high setting to secure the veneer in place.

Another gluing technique used by professionals is to continually check the project for square and alignment during the gluing process, including after the final clamping is completed. If you don't need clamps to hold the parts together, remove any clamps you have used quite soon after the glue has set. At this time you will still be able to make slight adjustments for level and squareness before the glue gets too hard.

The open time—how long you can expose glue to the air before completing an assembly—is about 10 minutes for yellow glues. Both humidity and temperature affect gluing action. Low temperatures slow set-up time while high temperatures speed set-up time.

Clamping time in cold workshops during winter may need to be twice as long as those used during summer. Below certain critical points, cold temperatures can weaken joint strength because the glue can't form a continuous film as it dries. If the temperature is too cold the glue may not work at all. For yellow aliphatic glues the minimum temperature is about 40° F.; for white polyvinyl acetate glues it is about 55° F.

Handling Glue Squeeze-Out

Once you apply pressure, some glue should squeeze out of the joint. If you don't have any squeeze-out it may mean that you are not applying enough glue and you will have starved glue joints. Be sure to remove the excess glue properly to avoid later problems in finishing. Spots of glue remaining on the surface will fill the pores of the wood. This will later prevent stain or other finishes from being absorbed by the wood and result in light-colored spots.

One way to remove excess glue is to use a damp sponge or rag right after it oozes out. The sponge or rag must be wet enough so that you can avoid applying a lot of pressure which can drive the glue into the wood. This method is frowned upon by many professional woodworkers, who say that a wet rag will only dilute the glue so it seals the wood to make it difficult to later apply an attractive, even finish.

A much better way is to wait until the glue has dried to the consistency of cottage cheese, then use a sharp paint scraper or chisel to remove it. But timing is important. If you scrape too soon, the glue will smear. If you wait too long, the glue will get too hard and you may chip the surface of the wood when trying to remove it.

Let excess glue skin over before removing. Waiting also lets the wood dry so it doesn't ball up during the removal process.

A small wood chisel can work well to remove excess glue from inside corners or next to moldings. Keep hands behind it.

A paint scraper does a good job of removing glue. If well-sharpened it will also take a slight shaving of the wood.

For glue residue on flat surfaces a good removal tool is a cabinet scraper. Always keep glue tools square to the wood.

To scrape off excess glue, first let the glue dry between 15 and 30 minutes, and regularly check the consistency of the excess glue. A good guide is to wait until the glue has formed a thick "skin" but still has a somewhat soft interior. If you wait too long on some woods, such as cherry, you will find that either a scraper or chisel may take off too many wood fibers along with the hardened glue. The timing for removing excess glue is not as critical with some other woods, such as oak or walnut.

Make certain that the scrapers or chisels you use are very sharp. If kept sharp, these tools will take off glue in ultra-thin shavings so you can easily tell when to stop without marring the wood. Touch up these tools often with a fine file. Or, if they are beginning to get quite dull, sharpen them with a hone or with a vertical 1″ belt grinder. After sharpening paint scraper blades on both the front and back edges, carefully use the shank of a screwdriver pressed against the front edge to slightly roll it over toward the rear (handle end) to get more of a "hook" on it.

Firmly press the scraper square to the surface of the wood and within a couple of swipes you should be able to get rid of most all of the excess glue. You will know if your scraper is properly sharpened if it takes off only a very fine layer of the wood along with the glue. Use the ½″-wide chisel to scrape the excess glue out of inside corners, or next to moldings. Cabinet scrapers can work well later to remove glue residue left on surfaces that are flat, and they will also help level out the joints.

Note: Respect the chisel's blade. Don't keep your free hand in front of the chisel in case of slips; keep it well behind the chisel, out of the danger zone.

If you have glued up pieces that are oversize, after gluing you can proceed to bring the wood to its final dimensions. Although excess glue should be removed in less than an hour after gluing, don't do any more processing of that wood until the glue and wood have dried completely. The reason for waiting is because the glue will swell the wood fibers slightly at the joints. If you begin to process the wood before the swelling goes down, you will remove some of these swollen fibers.

A minimum of three days at room temperature may be needed for complete drying. If some of the glue joints in your finished work are sunken below the wood surface, chances are good it was caused by working the wood too soon after gluing. If wood swollen from glue is planed too soon, more wood is removed near the glue line than on the rest of the surface. Then, though the surface may appear to be smooth at first, a

An old clothes iron can help glue veneer. Dampen veneer face, apply glue, and use the iron when glue is dry to the touch.

shallow channel can eventually develop along the glue line after it has dried out.

Finally, a word about storing your gluing tools. Gluing brushes will last a long time if you keep them immersed in water inside a recycled plastic container of your choice. In fact, the only reason you may need to replace the brushes is because the metal parts holding the bristles may begin to rust over time. Buying new brushes when you need them, however, will set you back only a few dollars.

GLUING CHALLENGES

Paying attention to gluing techniques can help you increase your project success. Often when problems occur it is the glue itself that takes the blame. However, the real cause may actually be linked to reasons besides the glue that was used, especially when working with previously-finished projects.

For example, if reglued wood joints are weak, the problem may actually be due to poor glue penetration. This problem is common when repairing furniture. It is very difficult, if not impossible, to reglue dirty joints or those filled with old glue. With the exception of some antiques, it is best to first dismantle and clean the joints, removing all of the old paint, wax, dust, oil, grease, and glue.

Warm vinegar will generally soften the most stubborn old glue. Dipping parts to be glued in warm water, and letting them dry completely, will help open the wood pores and allow the new glue to enter more freely. Warming the parts on top of a radiator, or in the sun, can also help open up the pores of the wood.

It is often a good idea to dismantle furniture to be repaired with glue. But some really old antiques, such as rung-type chairs and furniture held together with wooden pins or wedges, should not be taken apart. To repair loose joints in these, you can try to use a toothpick to work the glue into the joints. Or, you can drill a 1/16″ hole at an angle to, or alongside, the joints and force glue into them with a small oil can, a plastic squeeze bottle, or a specialty syringe.

Another situation requiring special consideration is gluing dowels. Some woodworkers put glue in the bottom of the hole and hope that when the dowel reaches the bottom the glue will be forced up around the dowel. For a good joint, a fluted or spiraled dowel must fit snugly enough to allow the glue to come up around it, the dowel must go to the bottom of the hole, and adequate glue must be used. The best way is to apply glue to both the sides of the hole and to the dowel itself.

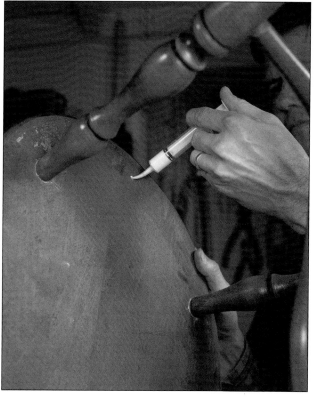

One way to re-glue antiques which you don't want to take apart: drill a small hole and then force glue into the joint.

Spiraled dowels should extend to the bottom of the hole and be snug enough so that they don't wobble in the hole.

SPLIT-BLOCK WALLS

*MODULAR BLOCK RETAINING WALLS
PROVIDE THE DO-IT-YOURSELFER
DESIGN & COST ADVANTAGES*

Modular split-face block retaining walls are popping up all over, and for good reason: They offer an attractive and economical alternative to conventional retaining wall materials, such as stone, concrete block, poured concrete, brick, railroad ties, and pressure-treated landscaping timbers.

For the do-it-yourselfer the interlocking blocks are a dream because of their relatively simple installation. Most of a retaining wall can be built with just one standard block without concrete footings or complicated foundations. The same basic block can be used to build just about anything you need, including straight, curved or serpentine walls, inside and outside corners, and even spiral, fan-shaped, or regular steps.

BUILT-IN ADVANTAGES

When set in place the blocks form a mortarless interlocking retaining wall that is hard to beat for stability and low maintenance. A big advantage for do-it-yourselfers is that each course is set back ¾″ automatically as the blocks are stacked to create a correct backward lean. With proper engineering, walls can be built up to about 40′ high. But walls up to 4′-high can be built without any special tie-backs or back-fill reinforcing. The result is a wall that is structurally sound and attractively blends into the surrounding landscape.

Within the industry the new concept is called "segmental retaining wall systems." Although there are several brands of the modular units on the market, all use specially configured blocks with a natural, split-face

New-style retaining wall systems are easy to install, and avoid many of the problems associated with other wall materials, such as eventual leaning and deterioration.

Though a number of tools are needed, the system doesn't require setting up forms for foundations or mixing any cement.

texture. And because all of the components are of concrete, this style of retaining wall gets high marks for environmental safety, which is not always true with other retaining wall materials.

One of the pioneers in this new approach to retaining walls is Versa-Lok, headquartered in Oakdale, Minnesota (see end of article for address). Engineers there emphasize that the technique can offer easy solutions to grade change and erosion problems, create more usable space, and spruce up your landscaping.

They also point out that a major advantage of building a retaining wall with these materials is that only a simple aggregate leveling pad is needed to distribute the retaining wall's weight. Because the units interlock with grooves and are installed without mortar, they can move slightly in relation to each other during freeze-thaw cycles to eliminate potential frost heaving. The dry-stacked units also allow water to move freely through the joints of the wall, preventing the build-up of water pressure behind the wall.

The basic wall units are not just concrete blocks with a split-face. They are trapezoidal shaped and are made of high-strength, low-absorption concrete available in *(continued on page 70)*

Successive courses of the wall are interlocked with built-in grooves, as well as the use of either nylon or fiberglass pins.

The blocks used in the system are pre-grooved from the factory for easy splitting in half to make wall corners.

The hydraulic splitter is energized by using a foot lever. Special cuts can be made with a diamond-blade saw.

1

Prepare a leveling pad by excavating and filling with a half foot of aggregate. Then position the screeding pipes.

2

Next, use your screeding pipes to help level the half-inch layer of fine sand spread out on top of the base aggregate.

5

After each block is placed into postion, you can use a torpedo level to check for level front to back and side to side.

6

Take time to level the first course. A four-foot level is a handy tool for checking how adjacent blocks match up.

3

Start to install the base course of blocks. If your wall will have a corner, it's best to start the first course at the corner.

4

Continue to add blocks to fill out the first course. The lifting device costs only about $40 and is well worth having.

7

For successive courses, align the blocks by sighting down the grooves on the top of each unit, or using a string line.

8

Place pins through holes of top block into slots of unit below. The next step is to install drainage fill and backfill.

Many suppliers of the split-face modular block systems offer helpful seminars, as well as one-on-one project consultations.

Walls of this type avoid the eventual leaning from water, soil, and frost pressure common with other wall materials.

(continued from page 67)

several colors. Versa-Lok units are available in gray, tan, dark brown, and rose. The units come with the specially-configured holes and slots that are molded in to accept non-corrosive nylon or fiberglass pins. As wall courses are installed, these pins are inserted through holes in the upper course and are received in slots of the blocks in the course below.

The standard Versa-Lok unit is 6″ high, 12″ deep, and measures 16″ across the front and 14″ across the back. Each weighs about 80 lbs. Though admittedly heavy, this weight helps increase the stability of the retaining wall. Special carrier devices available can make handling the blocks feasible for most do-it-yourselfers.

GETTING STARTED

The basic block used can be easily modified for an almost unlimited variety of wall designs, without having to order any special materials. Assuming you will have a level backfill and no excessive loading, you generally can build a 4′-high retaining wall without the need for professionally designed plans or special soil reinforcing. For higher walls, check with your supplier. The maximum height will vary with your particular site, the type of soil, and the loading conditions.

In most parts of the country, building permits are not required if the retaining wall will be 4′ high or less. However, always check with your local code officials before setting out to build your retaining wall. Also, before doing any digging, be sure to first confirm the location of any utility lines below grade.

The following tools can be helpful for building a wall of this type; many can be rented if needed: shovel, string line, line level, 4′ level, torpedo level, finishing trowel, sledge hammer, masonry chisel, brick hammer, tape measure, hand tamper, broom, goggles, vibrating plate compactor. A hydraulic splitter and diamond-blade concrete saw may also be needed, but they can be rented. Your supplier may also have the tools and may do the cuts for you or allow you to do it yourself.

Engineers at Versa-Lok suggest the following procedure for building a wall. Once you determine where you want your wall to be, lay out its location by driving a stake at both ends. Tie a string line between the stakes and, using a line level, take a reading at the midpoint to determine levelness. This will also show you how much excavation will be needed for the trench.

EXCAVATING & LEVELING
Excavate deep enough to accommodate both the leveling pad (6″ deep by 24″ wide) and the embedded blocks. The amount of block buried below grade is normally one-tenth the height of the exposed wall. For a 4′-high wall, for example, you would excavate approximately 12″ (the 6″ pad, plus one 6″-high unit). Additional excavation would be required for adverse site or soil conditions, such as soft or fill soils, steep slopes, or high ground water.

Prepare the leveling pad by placing 6″ of coarse-grained, well-draining granular material (sand and gravel or crushed stone) in the trench. Compact it to a smooth level surface using either a hand tamper or a vibrating-plate compactor. Then put a ½″ layer of fine sand on top of the leveling pad for final leveling.

To help prepare long, straight sections of leveling pad, you can create forms by leveling and staking metal tubing along both sides. Place and compact the leveling pad material up to within ½″ of the top of these forms. Add the sand and then screed off the excess. You are now ready to start laying up the wall.

BASE COURSE
Begin placing base course blocks on the prepared leveling pad. If there are corners in your layout, start laying units there and work away from the corners. Align the

units using the back edges and the slots on top to sight down. Front faces should fit tight and unit bottoms should be in total contact with the leveling pad. Level all blocks front to back, side to side, and with adjacent blocks. Remember that a level base course is critical; a minor unevenness at this point will multiply in succeeding courses and will be difficult to correct.

After the entire base course has been laid, place and compact the soil backfill (material originally removed from the trench) both in front of, and behind the embedded base course blocks.

ADDITIONAL COURSES
Continue laying the additional courses, being sure to sweep off any debris on blocks previously laid. Place this, and all following courses, so that the blocks set back ¾″ from the face of blocks installed below. The hole/slot pinning arrangement in blocks from Versa-Lok allows them to be laid in a variable bond pattern.

Whatever bond is used, be sure that vertical face joints are always tight to each other. Insert two pins through the front holes into the receiving slots in the lower course blocks. Use the outside holes when possible. If one is not usable, move the pin over to the next closest hole. The two pins used should engage two separate blocks in the lower course. If necessary, seat the pins by using a mallet and another pin.

Check the block alignment and level as you go. Depending on the length of your wall, you may need to install partial pieces to complete the wall. Create partial pieces by saw-cutting whole blocks as required.

COMPACTED BACKFILL
Stack no more than three courses before you backfill. Beginning at the level of the planned grade, place your drainage aggregate (¾″ angular gravel that is free-draining and clear of debris) directly behind blocks to a minimum of 12″. For walls over 3′ high, position a perforated, sloped drain pipe at the bottom of the drainage aggregate to collect and drain excess water.

The drainage aggregate is critical to wall performance because it keeps water pressure from building up behind the wall face. Next, place and thoroughly compact soil backfill directly behind the drainage aggregate. Place in 6″ lifts, compacting after each lift, using either the tamper or plate compactor.

Finish the wall by placing caps along the top. Two cap types are used in the Versa-Lok system—A and B. Alternate the A and B caps on straight walls. Use A caps for outside curves; B caps for inside curves. To adjust the spacing of caps on various radius curves, open or close the gap created by tapered sides on the caps.

Remember, though, that joints between caps should always remain tight at the front face. The front edge of caps may be placed flush, set back, or with a slight overhang. After all caps are positioned on the wall, cement them in place using an approved concrete retaining wall adhesive. Using two continuous ¼″ beads of adhesive placed along the top course blocks will secure the cap blocks. After the caps have been secured, all that is left is to finish the project with landscaping.

CURVES AND CORNERS

The general procedures for leveling pad preparation, drainage, and compaction are the same for curve or corner installations. Concave (inside) curves are built by increasing spaces between backs of adjacent blocks, always keeping front joints tightly aligned. Concave curves may be built at any radius, however a minimum radius of 6′ is recommended. (All distances are measured from circle centers to the front of block faces.)

Convex (outside) curves are built by decreasing spaces between backs of adjacent blocks. Since upper courses of the Versa-Lok units are set back from lower courses by ¾″, course radii become smaller as walls become taller. For a tight outside curve, you may have to cut the sides of several blocks to make the caps fit.

Outside 90° corners are easily created by splitting full-size blocks in half. These half blocks are then alternated at the corners with split faces showing. Half blocks do not pin; they should be secured with the recommended adhesive. No block modification is necessary to install 90° inside corners. Full-size blocks can be placed with faces showing to create an inside corner, adjusted for proper vertical joint arrangement.

Your supplier should be able to provide you with detailed spec sheets on installations, including how to handle curves and corners. Remember, before you begin to build any retaining wall, to always check with your supplier to confirm any technical details, planned procedures, specifications, or local codes.

Versa-Lok Retaining Wall Systems offers a variety of technical support materials. For more information and literature, you can write Versa-Lok, 6348 Hwy. 36, Suite 1, Oakdale, MN 55128. You can call 1-800-770-4525 or (651) 770-3166, or fax (651) 770-4089.

The beauty of the system is that it allows creative landscaping with curves, corners, steps, as well as serpentine patterns.

Modular block walls and front steps can add beauty and charm to your landscaping for relatively low life-cycle costs.

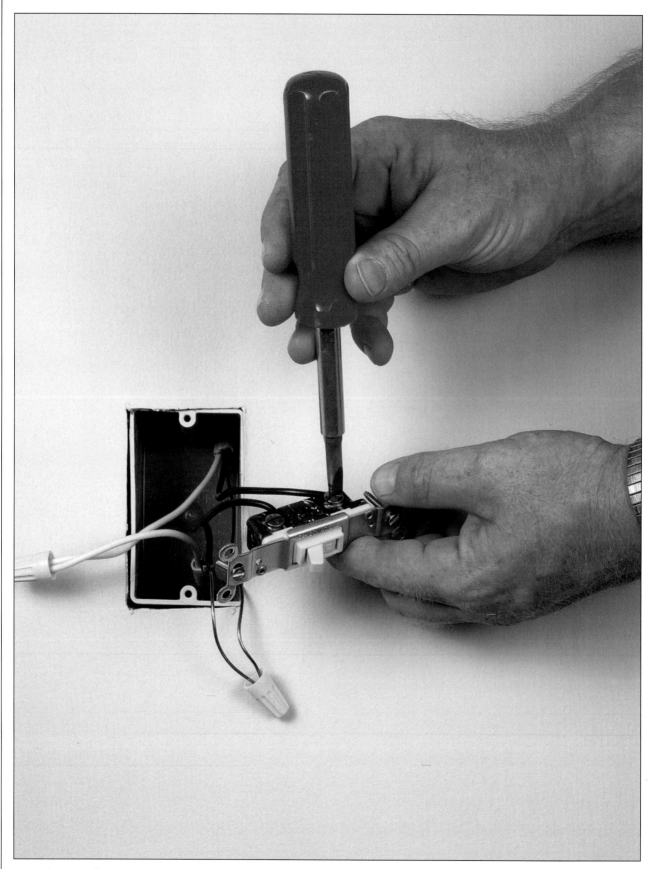

Switches must be removed for testing. Be sure to shut off the main power at the service panel, not just the circuit breaker.

SWITCH GLITCHES

HOW TO INSPECT & CORRECT FAULTY LIGHT SWITCHES INSIDE YOUR HOME

The lighting circuits in a typical home are remarkably reliable, especially when you consider how often they are used. But what do you do if a light won't go on, or you have to jiggle a switch to get it to work? Luckily, most light-circuit problems are easy to diagnose and also easy to correct. Here is a look at the five most common trouble spots.

Burned-Out Bulbs. When trouble-shooting a light circuit, start by changing the bulb to rule it out as the source of the problem. When a light bulb burns out, its wire filament breaks, interrupting the electrical continuity of the circuit. On occasion the filament burns but does not fall away, providing only intermittent contact inside the bulb, causing it to sometimes light and sometimes fail. Bad contact is a cause of light-circuit trouble that is easy to overlook.

Faulty Single-Pole Switches. Lighting-circuit problems most frequently occur in the switch. To check for switch failure, use an inexpensive continuity tester. First shut off the power at the service panel, and then remove the switch cover plate along with the mounting-bracket screws. Gently pull the switch out of the wall and loosen the terminal screws to release the wires. For stab-in connections, insert the end of a wire scrap into each release slot and push to free the wires.

With the switch disconnected, fasten the continuity-tester clip to one screw terminal and touch the other terminal with the probe. When the light switch is in the ON position, the tester's light should glow, indicating continuity. There should be no continuity, however, when the switch is in the OFF position. If the continuity test suggests that a problem exists, replace the light switch.

When you reinstall the switch, wrap the connector wires around the screw terminals in a clockwise direc-

After you are sure the power is off, then unscrew the switch cover plate and remove the switch from the electrical box.

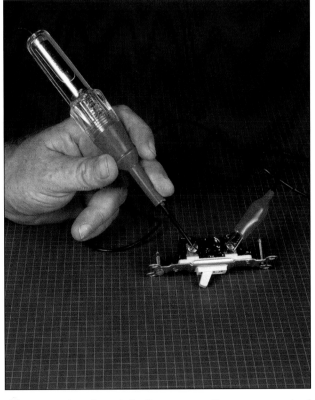

To test single-pole switch, fasten tester clip to one terminal and touch the tester's probe to the other, with switch ON.

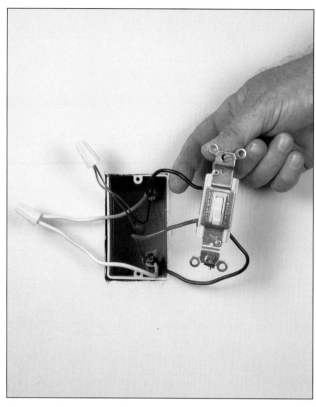

Notice the wiring of a three-way switch. The hot wire (shown over the index finger) goes to a common terminal.

tion. Then tighten each of the screws down securely.

Defective Three-Way Switch. When a light is controlled by two different wall switches, each is a three-way switch. Three-way switches are tested in a slightly different way than single-pole switches. In some cases, a light controlled by two switches may not work when either is turned on, so first you need to determine which of the two switches is faulty.

Start by turning off the power at the service panel and removing the switch cover plate. Note how the switch is wired—you will see three screw terminals. One of them, the "common" terminal, will be dark or copper colored. The incoming or outgoing hot wire, which is black, will be connected to it. The two other terminals will be silver; the wires connected to them are called "travelers," and they alternate current between switches. When you disconnect the light switch, tag the wire connected to the common terminal to avoid confusion.

Remove the switch and clamp the tester's clip to the common terminal, then touch the tester's probe to one of the two traveler terminals. If the tester doesn't glow, flip the toggle to the opposite position. If the tester still doesn't glow, the switch is faulty. But if the test

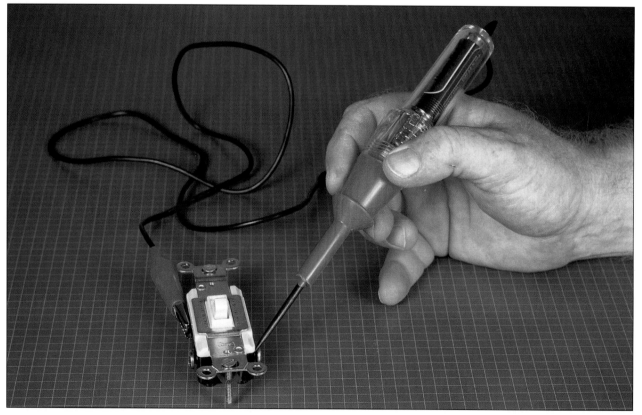

Test a three-way switch by fastening tester's clip to the common screw and then touching the probe to the traveler screws.

light does glow, move the probe to the other traveler and repeat the procedure. The tester's light should glow when the switch is flipped to the opposite position, indicating continuity. If it doesn't glow, the switch is defective and must be replaced. If the first switch checks out, reconnect it and test the other three-way switch in the circuit.

Loose Wire Connections. House vibration, caused most often by passing traffic, can loosen wire connections. Wires joined by wire connections (wire-nuts) are especially susceptible. Over the years, vibrations may cause a wire to back out of a connector, or a splice may be loosened enough to generate heat when current passes through it, creating a fire hazard.

A quick check of the wire connectors in the switch box and lighting-fixture box may reveal these problems. As always, start by shutting off the power at the main service panel.

Grasp each connector firmly and tug on the wires it connects. If you feel a loose wire, remove the old connector and twist on a new one. Connectors are color coded to indicate the number and size of wires they each can handle. Therefore, replace any connector with another of the same color.

If the wire ends are charred, as often happens when stranded wires from fixtures come loose, trim each wire and strip ½″ to ⅝″ of insulation from the ends. Then hold the wires together and make a new connection. With some wire nuts you should twist the wires together before screwing on the nut; with other special wire nuts you only need to keep the two wires together as the wire nut is screwed on. Check with your electrical parts supplier to see if the wire nuts you are using require the wires to be pre-twisted.

Faulty Fixture Sockets. Lighting fixtures are also susceptible to damage from vibration and heat. Vibrations can loosen a bulb in its socket; loose connections produce heat, which eventually weakens the spring-like center contact inside the socket.

To check the socket, shut off the power at the service panel and remove the bulb. Inside the socket you will see two soldered grommets that connect the fixture leads and the center contact. If the grommets appear loose when you move the fixture leads, replace the socket. If the grommets are tight, press on the center contact. If it flattens easily or is bent downward, the spring tension may have been weakened due to heat, and the socket should be replaced. However, if the contact still has plenty of spring in it, pull the tab up slightly and replace the bulb.

If you find charred wires, strip and re-splice wires using a new wire nut connector, pre-twisting wires if necessary.

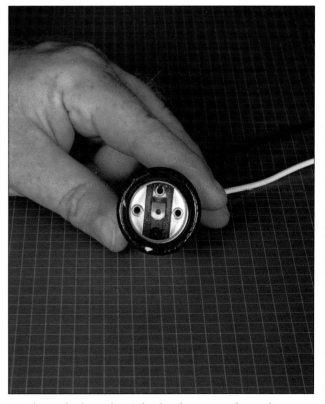

Look inside the socket. This head-on view shows the grommet connections, as well as the spring-tab center contact.

PACK-UP PICNIC TABLE

HOW TO BUILD A HANDY FOLDING TABLE THAT WORKS OUTSIDE OR IN YOUR HOME

This folding picnic or camp table makes a worthwhile accessory for outdoor activities. Big enough for a game of Ping-Pong, yet portable enough to put in the back of a pickup or mini-van, it can be just the ticket for family outings.

When fully assembled, the large table offers 32 sq. ft. of top area for picnics, working, or any for other use requiring flat-surface space. And, when the table is taken apart, the 4′ x 8′ top can be folded to a 4′ x 4′ size. The handles make it easy to transport it outdoors or inside to pack it away in a storage area.

Building the table is easy, and it only takes about six hours using a minimum of portable hand tools. The table shown is made from two sheets of 1″ APA marine-grade plywood, although with minor adjustments you could trade some sturdiness for lighter weight by using ¾″ material. Pieces of hardwood used for the wedges, in conjunction with the bottom support, hold the table tightly together. The hardwood dowels used between the two top sections of the table help achieve perfect alignment when it is set up.

CUTTING THE PARTS

First cut all parts for the table to proper dimensions. Lay out the large V-shaped cut on the bottom of one leg, and cut it out with a sabersaw. Sand the sawn edge. Use one leg as a pattern for the other. Lay out the 3″ radius at each corner of the table and cut them with the sabersaw. Next, lay out the two tenons on the ends of the stretcher and the 1″ radius notches in the

While designed with the outdoors in mind, this table can be pressed into indoor service in the rec room, workshop, or even the living room for family get-togethers.

The handy folding table is made from two sheets of plywood, and wooden dowels are used to help align its top halves.

stretchers, which make room for the hinges. Also make these saw cuts with the sabersaw.

Lay out the mortise slots in the legs and the wedge slots in the stretcher tenons. Cut each slot after you have drilled a hole in the slot for the sabersaw blade. Put scrap behind the pieces so the plywood doesn't splinter when the drill bit exits.

Use a scrap of 1″ plywood to test the width of the mortise slots in the legs. Adjust as necessary with a rasp and sandpaper. The stretcher tenons should slip easily into place, but not be so loose that they make the table unstable. After all of the components have been cut out, slightly chamfer the edges with a block plane and sand the chamfer to create a soft edge.

DOWELS & HINGES

Next, drill holes for three dowels using a doweling jig. Locate one dowel 2″ from each side and one in the middle. If the dowels aren't tapered at the ends, you can taper them slightly with a pencil sharpener so they will find the holes easier. Glue the dowels into one side of the table. You may need to wax the protruding part so they slide easily into the other half of the table top. Position the hinges onto the bottom, making sure they

Handles strategically placed on both sides help manuever the table when taken apart for either transport or storage.

Wedges of hardwood, in conjunction with the bottom support (stretcher), help to hold the folding table tightly together.

Three dowels in the center joint of the top halves guide the two parts into perfect alignment when the table is assembled.

Exploded View

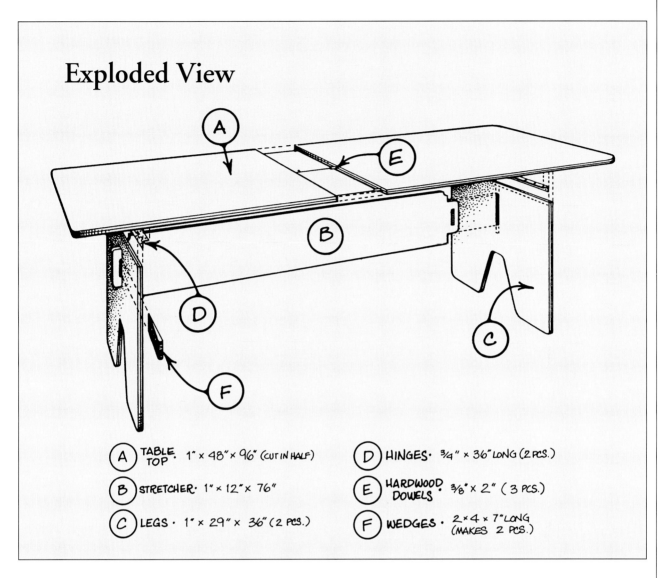

(A)	TABLE TOP. 1" × 48" × 96" (CUT IN HALF)		(D)	HINGES. ¾" × 36" LONG (2 PCS.)
(B)	STRETCHER. 1" × 12" × 76"		(E)	HARDWOOD DOWELS. ⅜" × 2" (3 PCS.)
(C)	LEGS. 1" × 29" × 36" (2 PCS.)		(F)	WEDGES. 2 × 4 × 7" LONG (MAKES 2 PCS.)

are square to the sides of the table. Attach them with ⅞" Phillips-head wood screws. Then screw the legs to the piano hinges. With a block plane, bevel the top edge of one leg as shown. This allows the leg to swing open a little more than 90° so you will have room to insert the table's stretcher.

Slightly bevel the leg, then swing it up and test to see if you can insert the stretcher. Remove a few shavings at a time until the tenon can be inserted without straining the piano hinge. If the hinge is repeatedly strained, the screws will eventually slip.

MAKING THE WEDGES

The wedges can be hardwood or a tight-grained soft-wood, such as Douglas fir. Start with a 1½" x 3⅜" x 7" block and saw it diagonally into two wedges. You can use a handsaw after you secure the block in a vise. Chamfer the edges with a block plane. A large chamfer

on the big end will prevent the wedge from splitting when it is tapped into place. Don't sharpen the small end to a point because a small flat is required to tap the wedge out of the slot. To keep them from splitting, soak the wedges overnight in boiled linseed oil and buff them dry with a soft cloth.

Before you finish the folding table, do a trial assembly to make sure that you have the proper clearances. Assemble the table upside down if you are working alone. Tap the wedges in just enough to draw the tenon shoulders snugly against the legs. Carefully flip the table upright. Support the tabletop firmly against the support board until the table is right-side up.

A variety of finishing options include a stabilized natural finish, a long-lasting pigmented finish, or an epoxy seal to improve abrasion resistance and water-proof the table. For a table that will see constant exposure, exterior enamel would be an excellent choice.

PACK-UP PICNIC TABLE
Bottom, Side & End Views

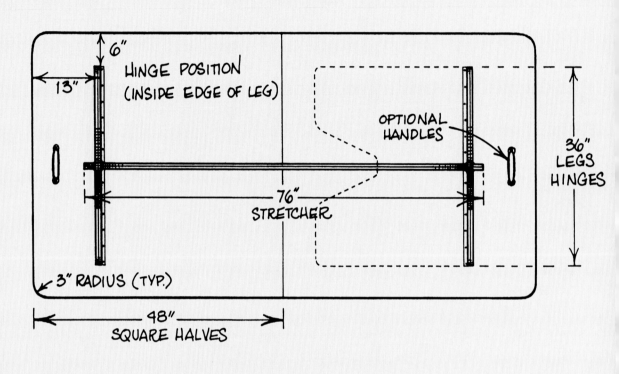

6"
13"
HINGE POSITION
(INSIDE EDGE OF LEG)
OPTIONAL HANDLES
36" LEGS HINGES
76" STRETCHER
3" RADIUS (TYP.)
48" SQUARE HALVES

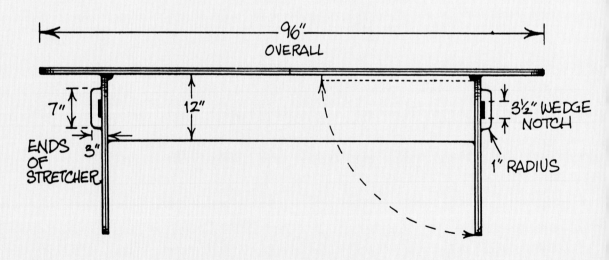

96" OVERALL
7"
12"
3½" WEDGE NOTCH
ENDS OF STRETCHER
3"
1" RADIUS

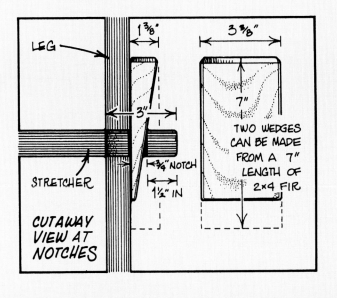

LEG

1 3/8"

3 3/8"

7"

TWO WEDGES
CAN BE MADE
FROM A 7"
LENGTH OF
2×4 FIR

3"

3/4" NOTCH

1 1/2" IN

STRETCHER

*CUTAWAY
VIEW AT
NOTCHES*

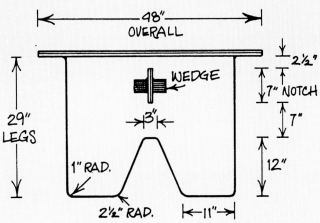

48"
OVERALL

WEDGE

2 1/2"

7" NOTCH

7"

29"
LEGS

3"

12"

1" RAD.

2 1/2" RAD.

11"

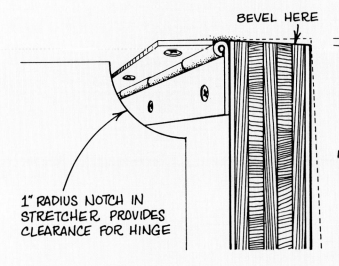

BEVEL HERE

2° TO 3°

1" RADIUS NOTCH IN
STRETCHER PROVIDES
CLEARANCE FOR HINGE

AFTER LEG IS POSITIONED &
HINGE IS ATTACHED TO TABLE,
PUT A 2° TO 3° BEVEL ON TOP
OUTER EDGE OF LEG......

THIS WILL ALLOW ROOM TO
INSERT THE STRETCHER TENON

SHINGLE REPAIRS

HOW MAKING SIMPLE REPAIRS ON DAMAGED ROOF SHINGLES CAN SAVE A MAJOR EXPENSE

Your roof protects every investment you have made in your home and its furnishings. So when a roof develops problems, everything under it is threatened.

When a roof is simply too old or too storm damaged to be repaired, there is really no alternative to a putting on a new roof. But with small, isolated shingle problems, there is no reason why you can't handle the job yourself. It doesn't take long for small problems to grow into big ones, so it is good to take care of them as soon as possible. With about $20 and a couple of hours of time, you can add years to the life of a slightly damaged roof.

ASSESSING THE REPAIRS

When is a roof worth repairing? It depends on the nature and the extent of the damage, and the overall condition of the composition shingles. When the shingles reach the magic age of 20 years old, they can become brittle and the corners can start to curl downward. At this age they can't stand much tinkering or traffic, so repairs are harder to make and may not last all that long. In this case, a new roof might be the better idea.

If you decide on replacing the entire roof, be aware that it is one job where a do-it-yourselfer can save some big money. However, it does take some planning, some muscle, and a few friends or relatives to get it done in a reasonable amount of time. If you re-roof be sure to update the attic venting, and also decide if you want to replace the rain gutter at the same time.

But if your roof is generally in pretty good shape—

Repairing problem shingles on your house takes only a few dollars in materials, plus some basic tools. Making shingle repairs promptly can potentially save you big money.

Reach under the damaged shingle to pry out the nails. If possible, lift tabs on the row above and pry out top four nails.

the shingles still lay flat and there are no leaks—then chances are good that you will be able to replace or repair scattered shingle problems and postpone what would have been a big dent in your bank account.

FLASHING OR ROOF?

A roof can develop problems in two general areas. The first is in individual shingles, usually because they were damaged before, during, or after the installation. The second most common problem is in the metal flashing around chimneys and flues or in valleys. Flashing problems can sometimes be fixed successfully with tar-based roofing sealant.

If that fails, then major repairs may be in order, such as replacing the flashing. In some cases the flashing was installed incorrectly to start out with. Faulty flashing can often lead to replacements of such expensive items as skylights, when the real problem was only how the flashing was installed. So before you tear into the roof and replace any part of the flashing, you should either do enough research on the subject to get it right, or hire a professional.

While the best time to replace flashing is when the roof is replaced, if the problem flashing extends only to a limited area you might be able to fix it. Sometimes a professional who is flashing-savvy will help you evaluate your present flashing and tell you how to correct it for a small fee. The other option, of course, is to have him do the job for you.

PROBLEMS & CAUSES

Individual shingles can fail either because of physical damage or factory defects. Factory defects seldom show up at the time of installation. The shingles may look good, but for some reason they age faster than the surrounding shingles. Some shingles may be scuffed or damaged in shipment or during installation. In these cases, corners may curl or splits may develop.

But probably the biggest cause of shingle damage is severe weather. High winds can rip the tabs from perfectly good shingles and falling tree branches can tear or scuff the shingles. In some cases a few shingles can be blown off the roof. Luckily, much of this type of damage can be repaired quickly and inexpensively, and with just basic hand tools.

In the photos shown here, there were several shingles which had tabs that were ripped off in a storm and some that were split by falling tree branches. There were also some shingles with a slight upward curl in the corners, likely the result of previous damage.

If you left the top four nails in place, cut notches in the top of the new shingle from the back side to fit around the nails.

STARTING THE JOB

The first thing to look for is replacement shingles. Finding exact replacements can be no problem or a big problem, depending on the age of your roof. If your shingles are still being made, just buy a bundle—one-third of a square—and use what you need. Save the rest for future use.

A bundle of common, three-tab asphalt or fiberglass shingles will cost you around $10. These new shingles will have a slightly different appearance until they weather for about a year. But eventually they should blend in with the rest of the roof.

If your shingle color is no longer available, your only choice will be to try to find something similar, even if it is from a different manufacturer. If you can't find something close at your home center or lumberyard, try a commercial roofing wholesaler. These companies usually have access to more brands and styles.

Beyond that, you will need a tube of tar-based roofing sealant (about $2), a few galvanized shingle nails, a caulk gun, pry bar, utility knife, and hammer.

Replacing a mid-roof shingle is not as difficult as you might think. Because shingles are layered, bottom to top, it may appear that you would need to tear off the shingle above to reach the damaged one. But that

In some cases you may need to cut a sliver from each of the sides of the new shingle so that it will easily slide in place.

Next, slide the new roof shingle under the existing upper shingle until the shingle's tabs are aligned with those next to it.

Then lift the tabs of the upper roof shingle to nail the new shingle in place. Sink one roofing nail above each tab slot.

To repair a shingle with a curled corner, apply a small daub of roofing sealant under the corner, then press down firmly.

is not the case. On a warm day all nails can be removed with a pry bar and a little patience. With the nails removed, the damaged shingle will slip right out.

Each shingle is nailed initially in four places, once on each end and once above each tab slot. But when the next row of shingles is installed, the nails used for that row will also catch the top of the lower shingle. As such, each shingle is nailed eight times, which can make the upper nails seem inaccessible. But you can get at them by lifting the tabs very carefully and sliding a pry bar under them.

To keep from damaging the upper shingles, use a putty knife or a 3″ drywall knife to free the tabs. Just slide the tool under each tab and pry gently. When the tabs break free of their sealer strip, you will see the first row of nails securing the damaged shingle. Slide the pry bar under the damaged shingle, against the first nail, and then pry it up.

In other words, use the shingle to lift the nail. When you see the nail lift out about a quarter inch, pull the pry bar from under the shingle and press the shingle down around the nail. Then pull the nail with the bar from above. Repeat this procedure with each of the four primary nails. Next, pry up the tabs on the next row above the damaged shingle and do the same.

Weight the curled corner down with a brick or a similar object to hold it flat. Remove the brick the following day.

To repair a split shingle tab without having to buy new shingles, apply a small bead of sealant under and over the split.

After the roofing sealant has been applied, the next step is to spread the sealant neatly over the tab using a putty knife.

3

To camouflage the black sealant over the tab split, sprinkle the sealant with color chips collected from your rain gutters.

Again, use the shingle under the nail head to lift the nail slightly, then pull the nails with the bar. With all eight nails removed, pull the damaged shingle out and discard it.

The only difference between the first and second row of nails is that you won't have as much room to work under the second row. Still, it is not difficult. It just takes patience and a relatively warm and pliable shingle. With enough warmth, the shingle will remain flexible enough so that when you stretch it to reach the nails, it will lay flat again in short order. If you need to do this work on a cold day, you can use a hair dryer or a heat gun to warm up the shingle.

HANDLING OLDER SHINGLES
With older, more brittle shingles, you may not want to risk pulling the second row of nails, for fear of breaking the upper shingle. In this case, tear off the damaged shingle near its upper nails and clean the debris from under the upper shingle. Then trim the replacement shingle to accommodate the four nails that remain in place. Just turn the new shingle over and cut V-notches above the tab slots.

When you have trimmed the new shingle to fit, carefully slide it in place under the upper shingle, until the tabs match those of the adjacent shingles. Finally, lift the tabs of the upper shingle and nail the new shingle in place, with one nail above each tab slot.

CURLED & SPLIT SHINGLES
When a shingle curls up on one corner, it is often because the corner was slightly crushed during shipment or on the job. In most cases it will lay down with the first warm day, but not always. If you notice a corner curling up, apply a small daub of roofing sealant under the corner. Then press the corner down firmly and weight it down with a brick for a day or so.

When a shingle tab is really broken, it is best to replace the entire shingle. But if the tab has only a small tear, or if you don't want to buy an entire bundle of shingles to make such a small repair, just apply a thin bead of sealant under and over the tear. Then smooth out the top bead with a putty knife.

With that done, look in your rain gutters for the usual accumulation of color chips that wash from the shingles. Gather some of these chips into a small cup and sprinkle the chips over the black bead until you have covered the sealant thoroughly. This is a stop-gap measure, but it does a reasonable job of hiding an otherwise conspicuous surface repair.

DRYER VENT UPGRADE

*AN EASY PROJECT TO HELP YOU
SAVE SPACE, INCREASE SAFETY &
BOOST YOUR DRYER'S EFFICIENCY*

If your dryer is vented with plastic or metal-foil exhaust piping, you may want to consider upgrading to a more sturdy system. The lightweight vent kits of the type that was probably used to vent your dryer are inexpensive and user-friendly. But they are really not the best option. In fact, they have proven so problematic that many building codes now ban them entirely.

Why are these venting arrangements so troublesome? First of all, plastic is a fire hazard on gas dryers. And more than a few feet of either plastic or metal-foil vent piping will greatly reduce the efficiency of any clothes dryer, either a gas or electric model.

The bellows-like, ribbed inner surface of these venting materials produces air turbulence, which in turn reduces air flow. When that moist hot air in your dryer is not expelled quickly and efficiently, the interior of your dryer will remain wetter longer. With this kind of back pressure it will simply take longer to dry your clothes, which means you will invest more money in every load that you run through the dryer.

Secondly, these venting arrangements also accumulate more lint, which can be a fire hazard. And in really inefficient installations they can even shorten the life of the dryer. A smooth metal vent, on other hand, creates very little air turbulence and resistance, and is therefore much more efficient.

The difference can be substantial. In real-life installations, professional installers report that replacing eight feet of plastic flex vent pipe with smooth metal vent

Replacing old plastic or metal-foil flexible venting pipe won't cost you much and will help cut the cost of drying clothes. Accessories available also can help you save space.

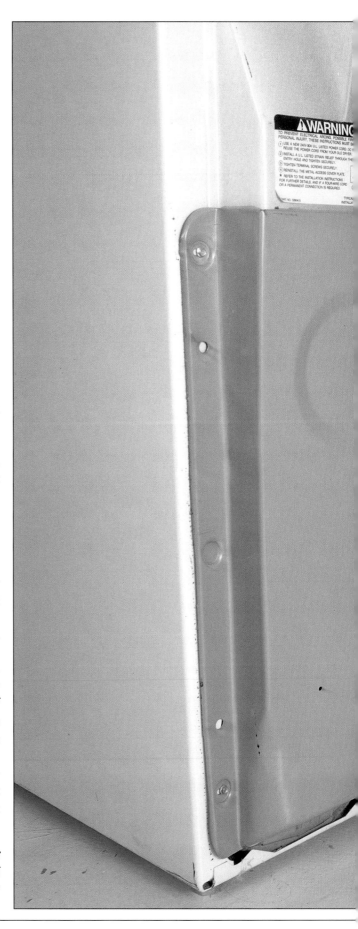

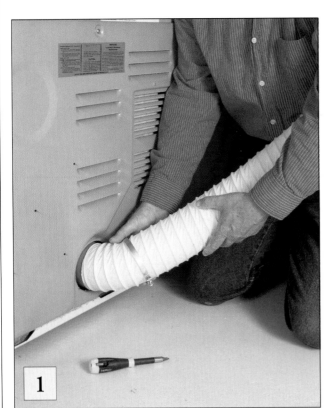

Loosen up the band clamp that secures the old plastic vent pipe to the dryer's exhaust outlet, then pull the pipe free.

Put a new band clamp over vent box's lower fitting. Slide the fitting over the dryer outlet and then tighten up clamp.

can shave nearly 10 minutes off of the time that it takes to dry a load of bath towels.

VENTING PRINCIPLES

The bottom line is that air flows most efficiently through smooth vent pipes with few turns. Every turn, and every surface irregularity, creates friction and turbulence. While most vent pipes will need to have a few turns, and some surface ridges are unavoidable, the goal is to keep them to a minimum.

In fact, building codes are fairly specific in this regard. The more turns you have in a vent pipe, the shorter the run must be. If you were to install a simple 4″ smooth metal vent pipe with only two 90° elbows, you could legally extend that vent pipe run to 38′, a distance that some home designs require. But add just two more elbows, and the maximum allowed length is cut down to 21′. Flexible metal vent in this situation would trim the allowable length to 15′.

VENTING OPTIONS

In the project shown here the goal was to replace older plastic flex vent piping with something more efficient, as well as to allow the dryer to be pushed farther back against the wall to allow more clearance in front. The most efficient approach would have been 4″ round metal vent pipe with two elbows, basically a straight vertical run between the back of the dryer and the permanent metal vent in the ceiling.

But to illustrate the advantage of a narrow box vent—which requires less space between the dryer and the wall—two Whirlpool vent kits were used. One was an adjustable periscope-type vent box that would clear the top of the dryer. The other was a kit with two lengths of heavy flexible metal vent pipe that would be used to connect the dryer to the overhead vent.

Whirlpool is one company that makes a variety of accessories for various venting configurations, including several for those tight-fit, upper-story laundry closets that are so popular today. The Whirlpool Dura Safe periscope vent box accessory used in the project was a 2″ deep x 6″ wide box that can adjust from 29″ to 52″ high. It cost about $20. The kit with the two lengths of Dura Safe round 4″ metal flex vent piping also cost about $20.

The Dura Safe metal flex vent piping can be lengthened somewhat and shaped to accommodate slight offsets. It would work fine in this installation because of the relatively short run, and it would be a safety improvement over the existing plastic piping. It comes

3

With the periscope box installed on the back of the dryer, extend it upward until its top fitting clears the dryer's panel.

To connect the flex pipe to the outside vent pipe in the ceiling, insert the male end of the elbow and secure with a clamp.

Next, position the lower flex vent pipe over the fitting on the outlet at the top of the adjustable periscope vent box.

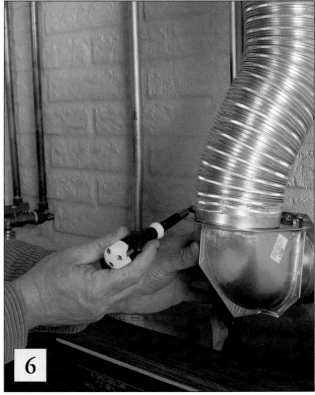

When positioned, secure the flex vent pipe to the periscope vent box using one of the clamps that come with the kit.

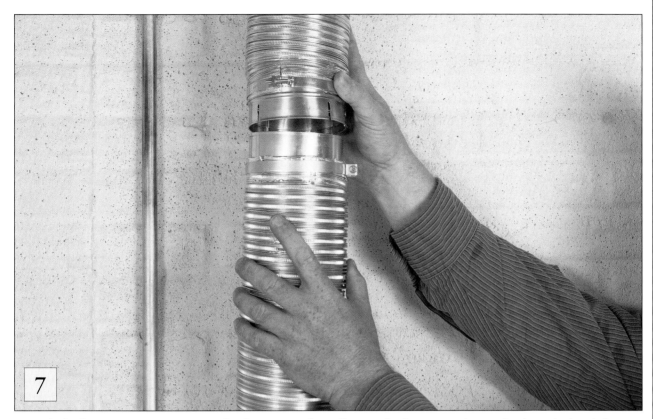

7

Stretch the flex pipe sections to meet each other against the wall, snap the fittings together, and tighten the band clamps.

with hard 90° elbows and band clamps for all connections. The external clamps eliminate the need for using screws which can catch lint.

GETTING STARTED

Begin by pulling the dryer out and disconnecting the power cord. Using a slotted screwdriver or nut driver, loosen the band clamp that secures the old plastic vent piping to the dryer's exhaust outlet. With the clamp loosened, pull the vent pipe from the outlet and clear away any lint you find there. Then disconnect the plastic pipe from the vent in the ceiling which runs to the outside. Again, lint often accumulates at sharp turns, so clear away any lint from this location.

To install the telescoping vent box—the periscope—slide a metal band clamp over the lower vent pipe fitting and slide this fitting over the dryer's exhaust outlet. While holding the vent pipe in place, tighten the clamp until it feels snug. Then slide the upper two sections of the periscope upward until the top fitting extends above the back of the dryer. While holding the periscope in place, reconnect the power cord and slide the dryer back against the wall. Sandwiched between the dryer and wall, the periscope should now stay in position on its own.

ATTACHING THE PIPES

This leaves only the two flex vent pipe sections to splice between the periscope and the overhead metal vent pipe. Starting with the ceiling connection, slip a band clamp onto the overhead vent pipe and insert the male end of the 90° elbow into this pipe. Slide the clamp against the elbow and tighten the clamp screw until it feels snug. Then extend the vent downward by stretching it as needed, and shape it to fit tightly against the wall.

Next attach the lower flex vent to the periscope fitting and secure it with a band clamp. Finally, stretch the lower flex vent pipe to meet the upper vent pipe and join the two. The ends of these vent pipes are fitted with metal slip-fit connections, so it is just a matter of snapping them together. The band clamps are used only to secure the fittings to the flex pipe.

When you have all the connections made and tightened down, then straighten the entire assembly and check for air leaks by operating the dryer and feeling with your hand around each of the connections. For more information on dryer venting accessories you can contact Whirlpool Corporation at 2000 M-63 North, Mail Drop 3004, Benton Harbor, MI 49022, or call 1-800-442-9991.

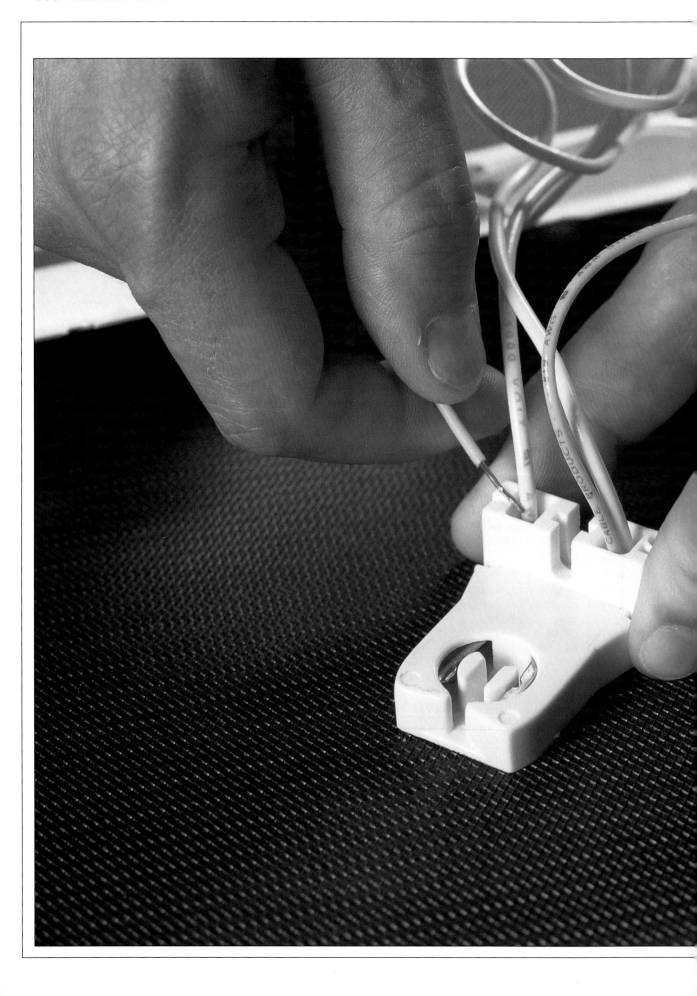

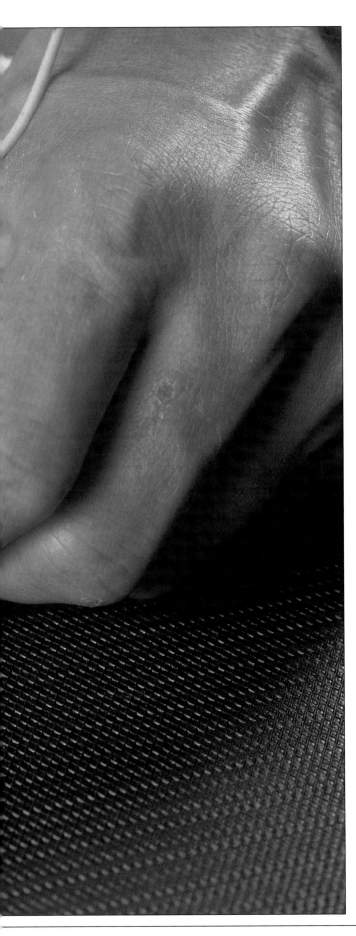

ELECTRICAL CLINIC

*A STEP-BY-STEP GUIDE ON
HOW TO ADD A DIMMING SWITCH
TO FLUORESCENT FIXTURES*

While variable-brightness fluorescent lights have been used commercially for years, few homes have been fitted with dimmable fluorescent fixtures. In fact, generally homeowners don't even know that this possibility exists for lighting in the home.

However, dimmable fixtures offer more lighting options, both practically and esthetically. Lights operated at less than full power save energy. A dimmable overhead fluorescent fixture can be used for task lighting one minute and for mood lighting the next. And you can convert a single fixture, or even gang several fixtures together for dimming possibilities.

PROJECT REQUIREMENTS

The conversion involves installing a dimmable fluorescent switch and a special ballast in the fixture. In most cases a new three-wire cable will also have to be installed, running from the switch to the fixture.

In the project shown here an existing two-lamp ceiling fixture was converted using a Hi-Lume switch and ballast from Lutron Electronics Co., 7200 Suter Rd., Coopersburg, PA 18036. Because compatibility between switch and ballast is critical, it is important to use the same brand components.

While there is nothing particularly difficult about converting a fluorescent fixture, the biggest challenge can be the required three-wire cable running between the switch and the ceiling box. Some switch circuits may already have three wires, but most do not. Installing the cable will be more of a challenge if you do

Re-wiring the fixture's sockets is part of the conversion to a dimmer switch. The project allows you to add custom control to the fluorescent fixtures in your home.

The first step in a project like this is to remove the diffuser of the fixture by lifting one side and bending it out slightly.

The tubes in the fixture were the rotated until socket pins were visible from below, then were pulled down carefully.

not have attic access, such as when the fixture is located on the lower floor of a two-story home.

However, there is always a way to fish cable through finished walls and ceilings. In some cases you may be able to pull the new electrical cable using the old cable if the staples holding the old cable will pull loose under pressure. Another option to get a new electrical cable in place is to cut out some of the drywall or plaster where the wall meets the ceiling. This course of action will require some repair work later.

STARTING THE PROJECT

The very first step of this project was to make sure that the power was shut off at the service panel. Besides insuring personal safety, turning off the power would protect the new components. Wiring them "hot" could result in damage that would void the warranty.

After turning off the power, the next step was to remove the fixture's diffuser and take out the lamps. With that done, the channel cover which conceals the ballast and socket wiring of the fixture was removed by squeezing the sides of the cover until they cleared the support tabs of the channel.

Next, the lead wires were pulled from the ceiling box and the wire connectors were taken off. Then the in-

The next step of the project was to squeeze the sides of the old fluorescent fixture's metal cover to release it from its tabs.

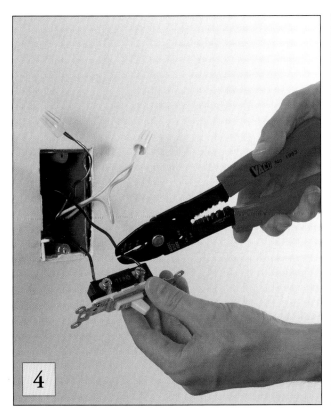

The old switch was removed. It can be done by either clipping the wires closely, or else by undoing the switch screws.

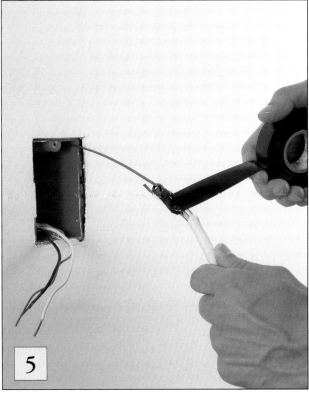

A fish tape was pushed through the switch box from the attic and then attached to the new cable with plastic tape.

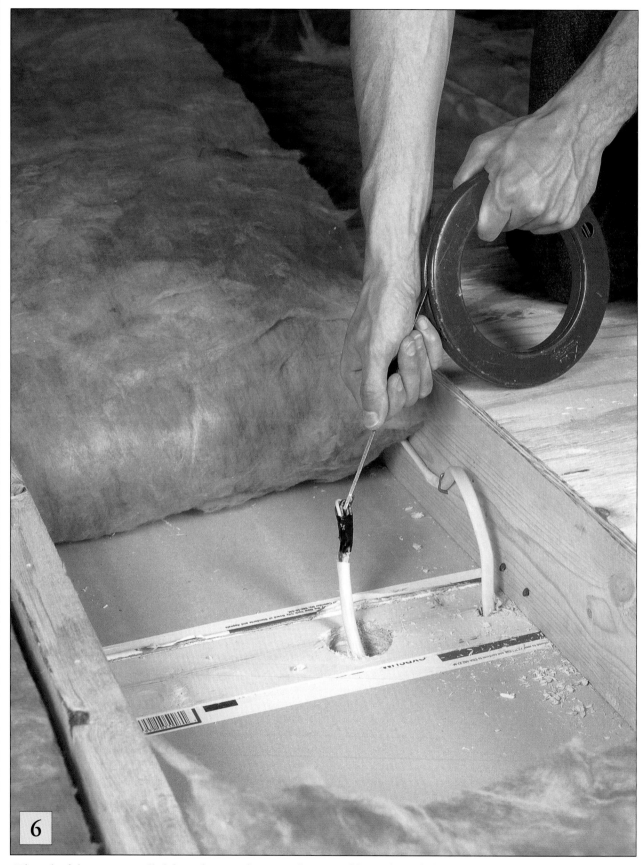

6

Then the fish tape was pulled from the attic, bringing the new cable up through the wall and over to the ceiling box.

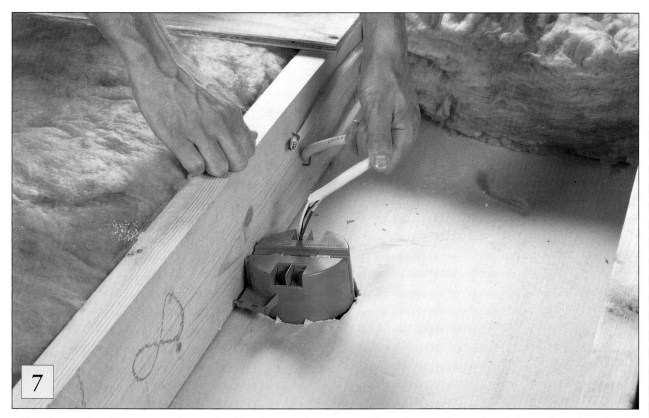

Abandoning the old two-wire electrical cable, the new three-wire cable with ground was then fed into the ceiling box.

coming wires were pushed through the top of the box to get them out of the way.

With the fixture ready, the next step was to move back to the switch box. The cover plate was removed, then the switch's yoke screws were unscrewed from the box. The switch was pulled away from the box and the wires were clipped close to their switch connections.

INSTALLING NEW CABLE

Dimming ballasts require three-wire switch legs. In this project the power originated at the switch and continued to the ceiling box through a 14 gauge cable with two wires and ground. This cable was abandoned and a 14-gauge cable with three wires and ground was fished through in its place.

Fishing the new cable through was relatively easy in this project because the attic was accessible. An over-sized 1½" hole was drilled in the top plate of the switch wall. Then a flashlight was aimed through the hole and the fish tape was carefully fed through one of the switch box openings.

(An alternative method would be to use two fish tapes and catch one with the other. One tape could be fed up through the box, with another fed down through the top of the wall.)

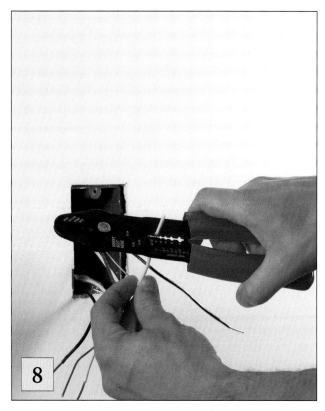

Next, about ⅝" of insulation was stripped away from each of the wires using an electrician's multi-tool.

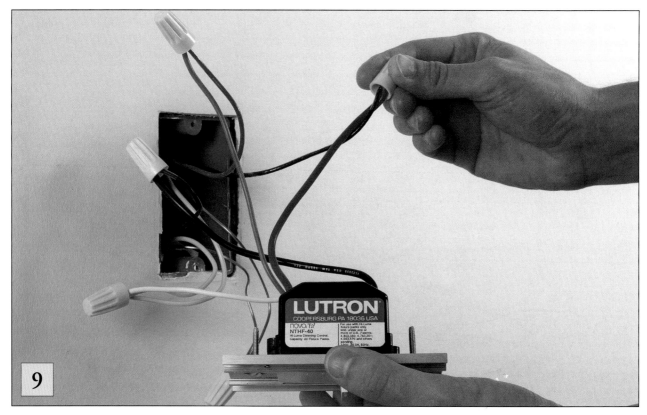

Next, new twist connectors were used to join the circuit wires, the switch-leg wires, and the color-coded switch leads.

All switch-related wires were tucked in the box, then the switch was mounted, tightening screws so the switch was snug.

After the fish tape had been fed from above into the existing switch box, the wires from the three-wire cable were hooked to the fish tape and secured with plastic tape. The fish tape and cable were pulled into the attic, then the cable was strung across the attic floor framing until it reached the fluorescent ceiling fixture box.

The cable was cut to length, allowing about a foot of cable to extend through the switch box and the ceiling box. About 10″ of sheathing was stripped from each end of the new cable, which was then stapled to the ceiling joists every 4′ and to within 8″ of the ceiling box. After inserting the stripped cable into the fixture box, it was time to return to the switch box to install the new switch.

INSTALLING THE SWITCH

Because different manufacturers have their own wiring configurations, the next step was to check the product literature carefully. The dimmer switch used for this project came with one orange lead, one red lead, one black lead, and one white (neutral) lead.

The installation was begun by stripping about ⅝″ of insulation from each of the switch box wires. Then the white lead was joined to the white circuit neutral and to the white switch-leg neutral. Next, the black switch lead was joined to the black circuit hot wire. All of the connections were made with twist connectors.

Since the switch used in this project did not have a grounding lead, the circuit ground and the switch-leg ground were joined and tucked into the box. To complete the wiring to the switch leg, the red switch lead was joined to the black switch-leg wire and the orange lead was joined to the red switch-leg wire. Then all wires were folded into the back of the box and the switch and cover plate were installed.

INSTALLING THE BALLAST

To install the new ballast, the lamp sockets were first slid inward to release them from their tabs, then the screws holding the old ballast were undone. The ballast and sockets were taken to a workbench so that the sockets could be connected to the new ballast.

To do this, the first job was to locate the spring-loaded, stab-in wire connections on the sockets and to carefully pull the old wires from their slots. Then ½″ of insulation was stripped from the new wires before they were pressed into the slots.

Because each ballast/socket wire is color-coded, the easiest approach was to simply duplicate the wiring of the old ballast. In this case the red and blue wires

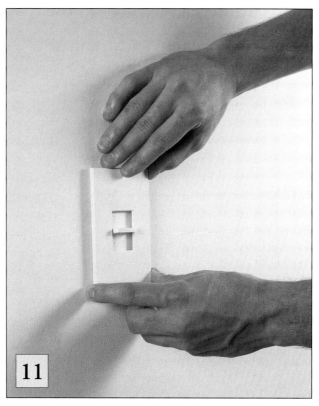

11

To finish, the flexible-plastic cover plate for the new dimmer switch was snapped over the sides of the switch yoke.

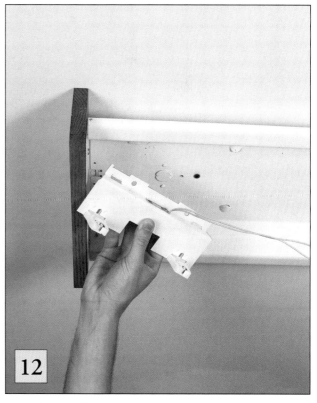

12

The fixture's lamp sockets were then removed by simply pulling inward until the sockets cleared their channel tabs.

Next, the old ballast was removed by loosening the holding screws that secured it to the metal channel inside the fixture.

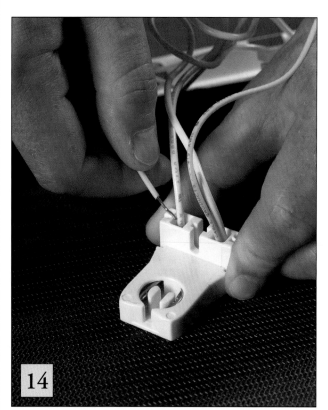

The old wires were carefully pulled out of the socket stab-in connectors and the new ballast wires were pushed in.

served the sockets on one end of the fixture, and the yellow and white wires served the opposite end. To keep from cross-wiring the sockets, each four-wire set was completed before going on to the next.

After the sockets were wired to the new ballast, the entire assembly was lifted to the fixture and the sockets were slid back under their tabs. Then the new ballast was attached to the fixture channel. The new ballast used in this project was longer than the old one, so a pilot hole was drilled in the channel to accept one of the mounting screws.

FINISHING THE PROJECT

After the ballast was in place, the next step was to make the wiring connections according to the manufacturer's instructions. In this project this was begun by connecting the circuit ground (bare) wire to the insulated green wire already bonded to the metal fixture. Then the wires were joined white to white, black to black, and orange to red.

With the ballast wired, all leads were tucked into the ceiling box and the channel cover was replaced, making certain all socket wires were safely under the cover. The last step was to reinstall the lamps and diffuser into the fixture, and then restore the power at the service box.

After the sockets were installed, the new ballast was screwed to the fixture channel, tapping in one new pilot hole.

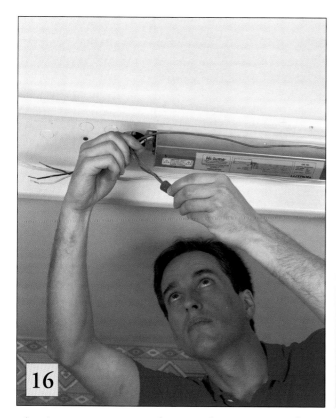

A twist connector was used to join the circuit ground wire to the insulated ground lead bonded to the channel.

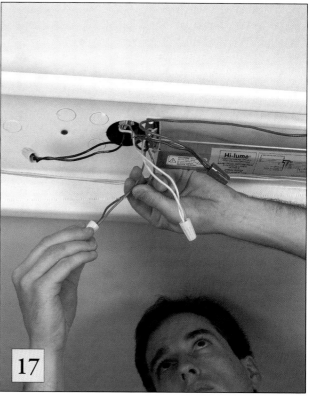

The ballast wiring was completed in this case by wiring white to white, black to black, and red to orange.

CAULKING QUICK-GUIDE

TRICKS ON HOW TO GET
THE BEST JOB OF CAULKING
DONE ON YOUR HOME'S EXTERIOR

Using a few tubes of caulk to further weatherproof your home will return its cost many times over. In fact, it is one of the highest-payback do-it-yourself projects that you can tackle. With caulk that only costs about $3 a tube, you will be able to seal up your home against air infiltration that wastes energy dollars.

The caulking will help stop air infiltration before it reaches your home's insulation buffer. The biggest opportunities are to seal openings that pass plumbing, ventilation, and electrical lines through exterior walls. Gas lines, phone cables, dryer vents, and air-conditioner lines are examples, but don't overlook exterior light fixtures and electrical receptacles. When buying caulk, go for the more expensive to gain a longer service life.

Start your caulking project by carefully inspecting the exterior of your home. Look for cracked existing caulk and any obvious service openings. Cut the applicator tip to a 30° angle and let the nozzle form a neat uniform bead.

When replacing cracked or separated caulk from siding seams, first cut the old caulk away. A carpet knife can work well. Slice into the joint from both directions with its hook-like blade, then try to lift out the old bead intact.

With older wood siding, paint supporting the caulk may also lift off. Before caulking a new bead, it is best to paint the joint with a high-quality exterior primer. Primer offers better adhesion than either top-coat paint or bare wood.

Take extra measures, if needed, on any flat-surface fixture or vent that spans lapped or grooved siding. With lap siding it is possible to splice a plastic or wood adapter, or at least a shim, if necessary between the fixture and siding.

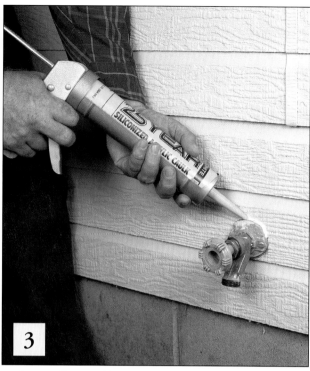

When caulking cables or piping, run a bead into the joint until it is sealed. Hold the gun at a 45° angle and feed in just enough to make a uniform bead. Avoid going over a joint twice; do touch-ups after the first application has set.

After allowing the primed areas to dry at least for a day, recaulk the seam with a flexible, exterior-grade caulk. Resist the temptation to smooth joints with your finger; this can produce thin edges which can lose their surface grip.

After the new caulk has set long enough for it to skin over, roughly in about half hour, you can proceed to re-paint the joint, caulk and all, with a top-coat paint. This should produce a caulking job that is relatively inconspicuous.

WALLPAPER REPAIRS

*SLICK WAYS TO FIX THOSE
BUBBLES, LOOSE SEAMS, TEARS
& PUNCTURES ON YOUR WALLS*

Wallpaper is a great way to dress up a room, but like every other surface in a home, it can take a beating. Chairs tip against it, hands and blue jeans scuff its seams, and all manner of indoor high jinks leave their mark.

That's the bad news. The good news is that most minor damage can be repaired fairly easily. Simple repairs can be managed with a few tools and a tube of seam adhesive, while larger repairs might require a scrap of left-over wallpaper and some spackling. In any case, this is work you can do and, in the bargain, it will add years to the life of your wallpaper.

COMMON PROBLEMS

The three most common problems are bubbles, punctures and tears, and lifted seams. Bubbles in wallpaper are almost always an installation problem. Most often a speck of dirt or a paint chip will keep the wallpaper from laying flat during installation, and with time and humidity a larger bubble will form. In other cases, the wallpaper hanger simply didn't get all of the air swept out. Either way, the only approach is to open the bubble to release the air.

As for punctures and tears, they almost always require patching, either by replacing the entire strip or by cutting out a small section and splicing in a replacement piece. Wallpaper seams can let go for several rea-

Only a few tools and techniques are needed to get your wallpaper looking like new. Try to make wallpaper repairs as invisible as possible by working slowly and carefully.

To gain access to an air bubble that is marring wallpaper, first cut a quarter-inch vertical slit with a sharp razor knife.

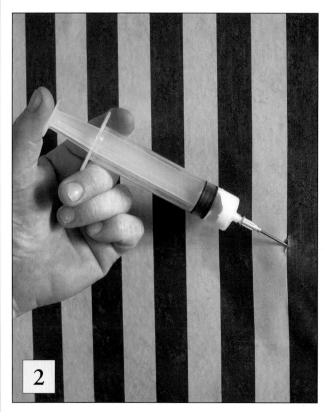

Use a paste-injector syringe to pump seam adhesive into the bubble. Then smooth it to remove the excess adhesive.

sons. Factory wallpaper paste doesn't stick well to vinyl, so an overlapping vinyl seam, or one that has had too much of the paste squeezed from under it, can lose its grip. Abrasion, which is common on corners in most rooms that are heavily used, can also eventually peel back a wallpaper seam.

WALLPAPER BUBBLES

Most bubbles are just air pockets, but it pays to check first. Press a finger against the bubble. If you feel a speck of some kind underneath the wallpaper the best approach is to cut an X-pattern over the speck and then remove it with tweezers or a knife. After that is done you then should be able to work seam adhesive into the cavity, squeeze out the excess adhesive, and seal the opening.

This basic approach works on a simple air bubble too, but for bubbles which are just air pockets a paste-injecting syringe is less intrusive and quicker to use. These syringes can be found at wallpaper and paint outlets. The syringe shown in the photo was purchased at a Sherwin Williams paint store for less than $6. It was made by Advance Equipment Co., 4615 West Chicago Ave., Chicago, IL 60651.

After you have a syringe, load it with seam adhesive

To fix a lifted seam, apply seam adhesive with a small brush. Then press the seam down and wipe away excess adhesive.

and push it directly into the bubble. With vinyl paper, however, the large needle may stretch the vinyl slightly. Considering this, it may help to cut an access opening. Cut a neat quarter-inch slit in the upper half of the bubble using a razor blade. Then pump in the seam adhesive with the syringe. After you have enough adhesive inside, squeeze the air and excess adhesive out through the slit and smooth it over.

LIFTED WALLPAPER SEAMS

The nice thing about working with lifted seams is that they are accessible. The only variation is whether they are also torn laterally. Small tears require a little more attention, but the repair procedure is still pretty basic. Begin by dipping a small artist's brush into seam adhesive and coat the underside of the exposed paper, top to bottom. A 4-oz. tube of the adhesive will only set you back about $3.

If you see a small ragged horizontal tear while making the repair, try to determine which side of the tear should lay over the other. If you lap the color side—the surface vinyl—over the white backing, you should be able to keep the white edge from showing when you are finished. In any case, press the raised seam down lightly with a finger and then wipe away any excess ad-

Next, use the seam roller to smooth the seam to the wall. Wipe the entire repair area with a clean, damp sponge.

Tape the repair piece over the damaged section. Then use a straightedge and a razor knife to cut through both the layers.

Next, start in one corner of the cut-out area and carefully peel away the original layer of the damaged wallpaper.

hesive with a damp sponge. Follow up by using a seam roller to flatten out the seam.

FIXING PUNCTURES

As mentioned earlier, puncture damage almost always means a repair patch, which requires that you have a piece of the wallpaper saved somewhere. If you have a remnant, making a seamless patch is pretty simple. You will need to work carefully, but it is not difficult.

To create a patch which will be the exact same size as the piece removed, and one that will match your wallpaper's pattern, you can use the double-cut method. Just tape a piece of new wallpaper over the damaged area so the patterns match. If you find that the wallpaper pattern can't be matched perfectly, don't panic.

Wallpaper will stretch slightly when it is applied, so it is not uncommon for the installed paper to have a slightly distorted pattern. The solution to this problem is to just split the discrepancy, side-to-side, trying to average it out. The new wallpaper patch will stretch a little after you have wet it, and chances are good that you will end up with a seamless fit and a very close pattern match.

With the patch taped over the damaged area, use a straightedge and a razor knife to cut through both lay-

Next use a putty knife to fill any voids with no-shrink vinyl spackling. Make it level and allow it to cure several hours.

ers of wallpaper. If your wallpaper has a linear pattern it will help to cut along a vertical line. If your paper's pattern contains light and dark lines, cutting through a light-colored line will make the seam less noticeable after it has dried. In any case, cut an approximate square, and make sure you cut through the corners completely.

FINISHING THE JOB

With the cut completed, remove the repair piece and set it aside. Then, starting with an upper corner, carefully peel the damaged section from the wall. It will leave behind some of its backing, so carefully remove this sticky fuzz with a sponge and warm water. If it doesn't come off with the first try, re-wet and try again. The hotter the water, the faster it will come off. Patch any divots in the wall with no-shrink vinyl spackling, letting it cure for several hours.

After the wall is ready, soak the repair piece in warm water for about 30 seconds, then book it by folding it over, paste side to paste side. Let it book in this fashion for about five minutes, then peel it apart and press it against the wall. Use your finger tips to align the edges and the pattern, then smooth it with a damp sponge.

Finally, rinse the sponge out well and then use it to thoroughly wipe away all of the excess paste.

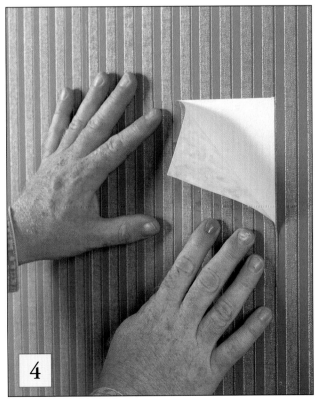

After wetting and booking the repair piece, apply it to the wall, aligning the edges and pattern with your fingers.

Sealing can be helpful for a new driveway poured in the fall, or whenever you begin to observe surface deterioration.

DRIVEWAY FIXES

HOW TO HELP YOUR CONCRETE DRIVEWAY LAST LONGER & LOOK BETTER

Concrete driveways overall have a good record of providing steady service for an economical cost. However, even a slab of concrete can deteriorate over time and lose its luster. To extend your driveway's service life, there are certain low-cost measures that you can take to keep it looking good for years.

FIXING CRACKS & JOINTS

One of the disadvantages of concrete is that it will eventually crack. The goal of masons who pour concrete is to try to confine the cracking to specific areas. They accomplish this goal by cutting in a control joint roughly every 10′ and installing an expansion joint at about every 30′.

To install a control joint a groove is cut across the slab, roughly a quarter of the depth of the pour. This effectively creates a weak spot, so any cracks resulting from traffic or ground movement will be encouraged to occur in the area of the control joint.

An expansion joint, on the other hand, is an oil-soaked fibrous joint that separates one side of the slab from another. This type of joint allows the slab to move slightly without causing the concrete to buckle under pressure. Expansion joint material, however, can break down over time. When it does, the slab is able to move laterally but doesn't move back, leaving a gap at both ends.

You can slow expansion joint deterioration by sealing the top of the joint. Sealing also keeps water and any resulting freezing from undermining the slab from below. You can seal the expansion joint with a commercial-grade urethane caulk that has both good adhesion and flexibility.

The joint shown in the photos was badly deteriorat-

Before sealing an expansion joint, dig all dirt and debris from the joint to stop deterioration and improve adhesion.

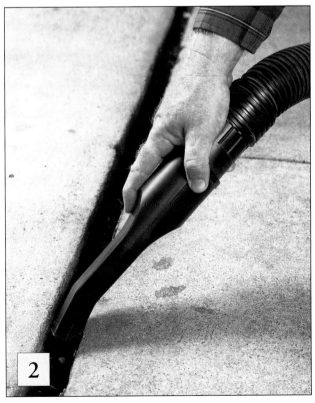

After digging as much dirt and debris out as possible from the expansion joint, use a shop vacuum to pick up the rest.

3

If a packing rod is needed, pack it into the expansion joint to bring the surface to a workable level for the caulk.

ed, had sunken nearly 2″, and had breaks in it. It was also covered with mud and leaves. Fixing it required two considerations. First, urethane caulk won't cure properly at thicknesses greater than ½″. Second, though non-flowable urethanes are available, self-leveling urethanes will flow through any gaps.

To bring this joint to a workable height, the dirt was cleared away and the original 1″ joint was packed with a 1¼″ backing rod held in place by friction. After the rod was pressed into the joint with a putty knife, each end of the joint was capped with a wooden stake to keep the caulk from running out the ends.

After the joint was ready, the top of the joint was pumped full of urethane caulk and allowed to flow into a level cap. It takes urethane a few days to cure properly. If you need to use the driveway within a few hours, it is best to sprinkle the caulk lightly with sand after it begins to skin over.

CLEANING OIL SPILLS

One of the most common driveway appearance problems, especially if you have older cars, is the oil spill from a leaky transmission or crankcase. You can remedy fresh oil-spill problems with common kitty litter.

4

Next, use a caulk gun to pump the urethane filler into the expansion joint. The urethane caulk will seek its own level.

Scoop out a general amount of the litter and pour it directly onto the oil spot. Allow the product time enough to absorb the oil. After the granules have turned dark, use your shop vacuum or a broom to sweep them up. Then sprinkle on a second helping and use a soft brick to grind the litter into the area.

Grind the litter into the spot using the brick in a steady circular motion. After the litter has been reduced to a fine powder and remains a light color, you will have removed all but a final residue that may cling to surface voids. This residue, however, will also be light in color.

If you don't have kitty litter, another product that will work on fresh oil spills is portland cement. For older oil spills, consider a commercial concrete cleaner or degreaser. You can get concrete cleaners at most home centers, and commercial degreasers are available from well-stocked concrete product dealers, auto supply stores, and swimming pool product outlets.

A good concrete cleaner will be non-corrosive, non-acidic, and biodegradable. Simply pour it on the affected area and use a stiff-bristle brush to scrub it in. After the grease has dissolved, hose the area down.

Kitty litter makes an excellent absorption material for freshly-spilled auto oil. Use a brick to grind in the litter.

SEALING THE DRIVE

Driveway sealants have gotten a questionable reputation because they are sometimes used by bunco artists involved in bilking homeowners out of cash. But they can be useful in certain situations. For example, when concrete is poured in late fall, a sealant can help keep water from entering the slab and popping the surface with the first freeze.

Considering using a sealant if your driveway is relatively new or if you see unusual surface degradation, especially if your driveway has a broom-finished surface. However, be aware that the longer a driveway goes without a sealant, the less likely it is to need one. The reason is that normal surface grime will help seal the concrete.

When buying a sealant, read the directions carefully. Most will require a clean surface and warm-weather application. Be aware that some may be incompatible with the curing agents used by some contractors, and that some may leave a slick surface when wet.

A resin-based clear sealant should cover about 125 square feet of surface per gallon. When applying a sealant, avoid using a paint roller or a spray gun which have a tendency to put it on too thick. Instead, brush the sealant in lightly, making certain that it doesn't puddle up on the surface.

For older stubborn oil spots, use a commercial degreaser. Brush it in until the area clears, then rinse off with water.

Building the portable shooting bench requires only a minimum of tools, and it comes apart in just a few minutes.

The bench, when folded, can be tucked behind the seat of your pickup, or even in the back seat of your car or van.

SHOOTING BENCH

HOW TO BUILD A HANDY
TAKE-APART SHOOTING BENCH
FROM ONE SHEET OF PLYWOOD

This folding shooting bench and its portable stool make it easy to sight in a rifle or scope. You will also find it handy for recreational shooting, providing you much more comfort than lying on the ground or draping yourself over a log to gain a steady position.

The bench is held together with a plywood support that fits through slots in the legs and is secured in place by hardwood wedges. When the wedges and support are removed, the legs, which are attached to the table with piano hinges, fold in flat and can be fastened to the top's underside with Velcro. The bench will come apart in minutes and will lay flat in the trunk of your car or behind the seat of your truck.

To sight-in rifles you can leave the target in position and then carry the portable bench away to the precise distance you want. This bench is equally useful for handguns or rifles, and offers a handy platform for ammunition, sandbags, a spotting scope, and other gear. It is stable on uneven terrain and becomes even more stable under the weight of sandbags and guns.

At home the bench can double as a handy table in the garage or workshop. One sheet of plywood is all you need to build both the bench and the stool. Both can be built with either ¾″ ABX or AB marine grade plywood. The ABX version will have a few small voids in the laminations, but it will cost less than the marine plywood which will be almost free of voids.

CUTTING OUT PARTS

First lay out all of the pieces on a sheet of plywood for cutting out. Use a sharp pencil and framing square. All of the 2″ radii can be scribed from the 4″-diameter lid of a 1-lb. coffee can. You will need a compass for the

(continued on page 127)

This three-legged bench, as well as the stool, can be made from a sheet of plywood to make sight-ins more comfortable.

(A) TABLE TOP • 1 PC. 3/4" × 34" × 40"

(B) RIGHT LEG • 1 PC. 3/4" × 29" × 32"

(C) LEFT LEG • 1 PC. 3/4" × 22" × 28 1/4"

(D) SHIM • 1 PC. 3/4" × 2" × 22"

(E) SUPPORT BOARD • 1 PC. 3/4" × 14" × 36"

(F) SUPPORT BOARD CLEATS • 4 PCS. 3/4" × 3/4" × 11"

(G) STOOL LEG (TOP) • 1 PC. 3/4" × 12" × 14"

(H) STOOL LEG (BOTTOM) • 1 PC. 3/4" × 12" × 14"

(I) STOOL SEAT • 1 PC. 3/4" × 13" DIAMETER

(J) HARDWOOD WEDGE • 2 PCS. 3/4-1" × 2" × 6-7"

(K) CONTINUOUS HINGE • 1 PC 22" LONG + 1 PC. 32" LONG

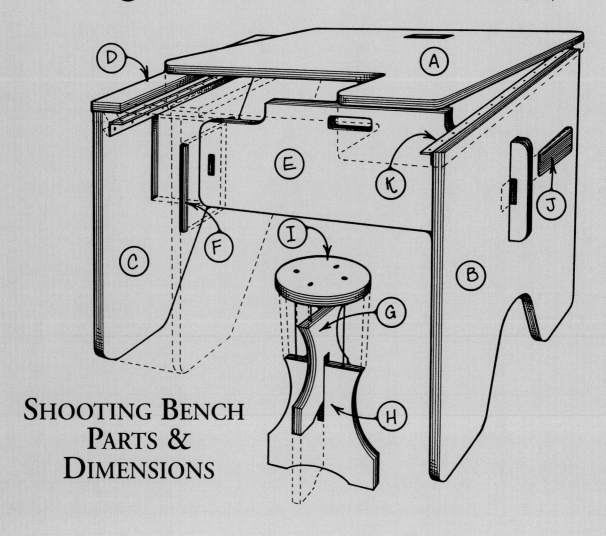

SHOOTING BENCH
PARTS &
DIMENSIONS

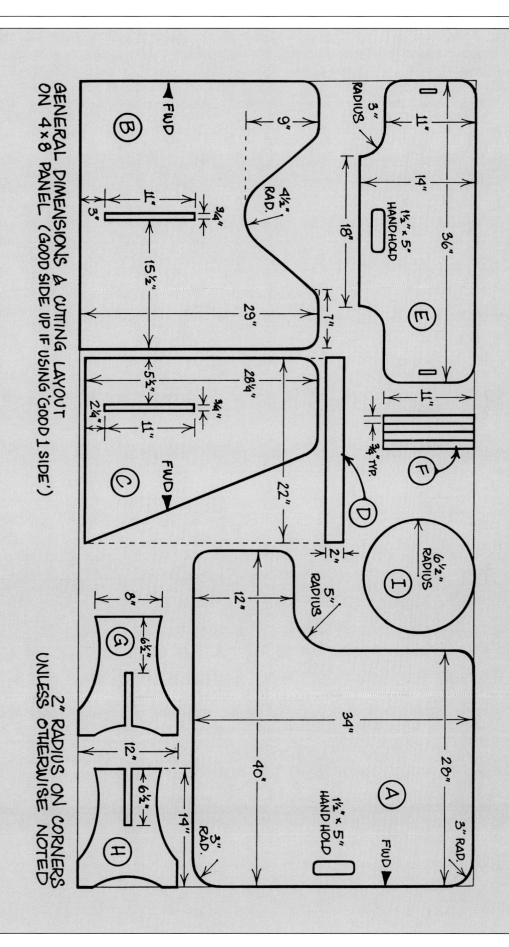

SUPPORT BOARD

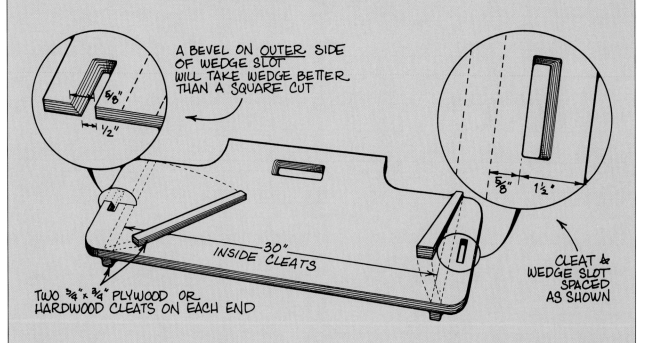

A BEVEL ON <u>OUTER</u> SIDE OF WEDGE SLOT WILL TAKE WEDGE BETTER THAN A SQUARE CUT

5/8"

1/2"

30"

INSIDE CLEATS

CLEAT & WEDGE SLOT SPACED AS SHOWN

5/8" 1 1/2"

TWO 3/4" x 3/4" PLYWOOD OR HARDWOOD CLEATS ON EACH END

LEG ASSEMBLY

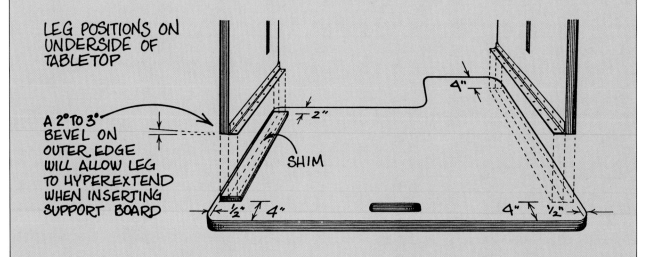

LEG POSITIONS ON UNDERSIDE OF TABLETOP

A 2° TO 3° BEVEL ON OUTER EDGE WILL ALLOW LEG TO HYPEREXTEND WHEN INSERTING SUPPORT BOARD

SHIM

2"

4"

1/2" 4"

4" 1/2"

(continued from page 123)

other curves. Use a sabersaw to cut the pieces, then smooth the edges by running a block plane over the straight edges. This will smooth any saw marks and bumps. Clean up the curves with files and sandpaper, then cut a very slight bevel on all of the edges with the block plane. Later use #60-grit sandpaper to produce a small round on all of the edges.

Next cut the slots and the hand-holds. The inside edge of all the slots and hand-holds are square to the surface, except for the wedge slots on the support board. Angle these wedge slots as shown for the support board slots.

Begin by marking all of the slot locations. Drill a ¼" hole in each slot to start the sabersaw blade. Clamp a scrap of wood under the slot before you drill so that the wood won't splinter when the bit exits.

Use a scrap of ¾" plywood to check the width of the leg slots. Then adjust the fit as necessary by rasping and sanding. Put the support board into the slot to make sure the slot is the right length. You shouldn't have to force the plywood in and out of the leg slots, but a sloppy fit will make the bench rest unstable.

The next job is to sand a slight round-over on all of the edges, including the slots and hand-holds. Then attach the cleats. The support-board cleats provide stops against which the legs are wedged. Fasten them securely with glue and screws to each side of the support board as shown in the drawings.

LEG ASSEMBLY

The legs are attached to the top with piano hinges, which allow them to fold in. Fasten a shim to the bottom of the table as shown with glue and screws. This shim, which is located under the left leg, lets the left leg fold over the right leg.

Attach the piano hinges to the bottom of the table and then attach the legs to the hinges. Use Phillips-head screws because the limited clearance may not let you hold the screwdriver exactly vertical as required for slotted screws. Plane a 2° or 3° bevel on the outside top edge of the left leg as shown to allow the leg to bend outward so you can insert the support board.

Put one end of the support board into the right slot. If you have trouble clearing the inside of the leg to get to the left slot, do not force the hinge. Just plane a little more off of the bevel on the top of the left leg.

Now make the wedges. First rip the wedges to the appropriate width on a tablesaw and do the rough shaping with a bandsaw or sabersaw. Use a block plane

A plywood support fits through the slots in the bench legs and is secured in place with the use of hardwood wedges.

to fine-tune the slope of the wedge and then bevel the top to prevent the wedge from splintering or splitting with use. Assemble the bench rest and test-fit the wedges. Work the dimensions of the wedges with a block plane until they fit.

Soak the wedges overnight in a penetrating oil, such as boiled linseed oil. You can form a small soaking trough out of aluminum foil for each wedge so that you can pour the oil back into the can later. After the soak, wipe the wedges off and wet-sand them with #400-grit sandpaper. Wipe and polish the wedges with a cloth until they are dry. More oil will bleed out of the wood later, so set the wedges aside overnight and polish them one more time before you use them.

To assemble the stool, slip the two sections of the stool together. The fit can be snug since you won't be disassembling it. Make sure the tops of both sections are snug. If not, plane the proud one flush. Put the stool's seat into position and pre-drill and countersink for 1½" wood screws. Then take the top off and put glue on the top edge of the base. Replace the stool seat and screw it into place.

Finally, apply the finish of your choice. You can seal the bench and stool with two coats of varnish. Your other options are to use paint or oil, as you prefer.

DREAM WORKSHOPS

*HOW TO SET UP YOUR OWN
HOME WORKSHOP FOR BOTH
ENJOYMENT & EFFICIENCY*

Who, among us who love tools and what can be done with them, hasn't dreamed about putting together a perfect workshop someday? Instead of having to deal with makeshift arrangements, we could pursue our projects in a dignified, organized fashion, and have room enough to handle projects of significance, like a livingroom full of furniture, that long-awaited wooden boat, the world's best garden gazebo, or restoring that '47 Ford pickup.

Setting up an efficient home workshop can be one of life's more pleasant challenges. On one hand it can be many times as involved as planning a bathroom, or even a conventional kitchen. On the other hand, setting up or improving a shop has some convenient advantages over other types of remodeling challenges.

GETTING SHOP IDEAS

Shop set-ups generally lack the sense of urgency involved when kitchens or bathrooms are torn up, disrupting your daily life. And they allow much more flexibility. You can arrange your workshop one way and, if it doesn't work quite right, you can change it around tomorrow, next month, next year, or whenever the time or the spirit moves you.

If you have been puzzling about how to set up a workshop, a good first move is to invest in an excellent reference book specifically on the subject. One such book is **The Home Workshop Planner**, available for

(continued on page 134)

When setting up a shop, consider adding all the weather-proofing amenities you have in your house, including insulation, attic vents, and heating and cooling equipment.

THE START-UP WORKSHOP (PAGE 135)

STAGE I TOOLS

- ❏ Circular saw ($75)
- ❏ Sabersaw ($50)
- ❏ Power drill, ⅜" ($45)
- ❏ Router ($75)
- ❏ Bench grinder ($65)
- ❏ Sander, pad ($50)
- ❏ Sander, palm grip ($60)
- ❏ Miter box, manual ($30)

TOTAL: $450

THE HOMEOWNER WORKSHOP (PAGE 135)

STAGE I TOOLS

- ❏ Circular saw ($100)
- ❏ Sabersaw ($75)
- ❏ Power drill, ⅜" ($60)
- ❏ Router ($100)
- ❏ Bench grinder ($85)
- ❏ Sander, pad ($60)
- ❏ Sander, palm grip ($75)
- ❏ Miter box, manual ($45)

Subtotal: $600

STAGE II TOOLS

- ❏ Tablesaw, benchtop ($150)
- ❏ Power miter saw ($135)
- ❏ Stapler/nailer ($30)
- ❏ Scrolling sabersaw ($50)
- ❏ Drill press, benchtop ($120)
- ❏ Belt sander 3x24" ($80)
- ❏ Air compressor ($215)
- ❏ Shop vacuum ($60)

Subtotal: $840

TOTAL: $1,440

WORKSHOP TOOL
BUYING GUIDE

HOW TO USE THE CHART

The chart summarizes possible approaches to developing a tool-buying strategy for the workshop you would eventually like to own. The chart's tool suggestions are intended as a guide, and the costs are based on retail prices. The chart is modular in several ways: 1) Successively complex workshops add additional tool groups and build on tool groups already purchased. For example, the array of Stage I tools purchased for the Start-Up Workshop are also used in each of the more complex workshops. 2) The quality and price of specific tools in each tool group increase going from less complex to more complete workshops. For example, the budget for the Stage I tool group starts with $450 for the Start-Up Workshop and increases progressively to a budget of $870 for the same tools seen under the Craftsman Workshop. 3) Depending on your needs and budget, mix and match tool groups or individual tools under the example shops for your own plan. For example, if you determine that the Woodworker Workshop is adequate for your needs, you could decide to buy lower-priced Stage I tools from the Start-Up Workshop, but may elect to invest in the higher-priced tools listed under Stage II of the Craftsman Workshop. The tools listed here can be supplemented with your choice of accessories suggested on page 132. Note that as stationary tools are added the duplicated benchtop tools can be sold or used for specialized purposes, as indicated by asterisks below:

*Benchtop tablesaw can be used for trimming large parts and cutting small parts during assembly. **Benchtop drill press can be used with sanding drums or for horizontal boring. *** Benchtop bandsaw can be used for small projects.

THE WOODWORKER WORKSHOP (PAGE 137)

- ❏ Circular saw ($125)
- ❏ Sabersaw ($75)
- ❏ Power drill, ⅜" ($75)
- ❏ Router ($135)
- ❏ Bench grinder ($100)
- ❏ Sander, pad ($75)
- ❏ Sander, palm grip ($85)
- ❏ Miter box, manual ($60)

Subtotal: $730

- ❏ Tablesaw, benchtop* ($200)
- ❏ Power miter saw ($150)
- ❏ Stapler/nailer ($45)
- ❏ Scrolling sabersaw ($80)
- ❏ Drill press, benchtop** ($180)
- ❏ Belt sander 3x24" ($90)
- ❏ Air compressor ($250)
- ❏ Shop vacuum ($100)

Subtotal: $1,095

STAGE III TOOLS

- ❏ Tablesaw, stationary ($600)
- ❏ Scrollsaw ($250)
- ❏ Bandsaw, benchtop ($140)
- ❏ Drill press, floor model ($300)
- ❏ Belt/disc sander, 4" ($120)
- ❏ Jointer ($300)
- ❏ Air tool set ($80)
- ❏ Drill/driver, cordless ($120)

Subtotal: $1,910

TOTAL: $3,735

THE CRAFTSMAN WORKSHOP (PAGE 139)

- ❏ Circular saw ($145)
- ❏ Sabersaw ($90)
- ❏ Power drill, ⅜" ($85)
- ❏ Router ($180)
- ❏ Bench grinder ($125)
- ❏ Sander, pad ($80)
- ❏ Sander, palm grip ($95)
- ❏ Miter box, manual ($70)

Subtotal: $870

- ❏ Tablesaw, benchtop* ($225)
- ❏ Power miter saw ($225)
- ❏ Stapler/nailer ($45)
- ❏ Scrolling sabersaw ($100)
- ❏ Drill press, benchtop** ($220)
- ❏ Belt sander 3x24" ($125)
- ❏ Air compressor ($275)
- ❏ Shop vacuum ($125)

Subtotal: $1,340

- ❏ Tablesaw, stationary ($850)
- ❏ Scrollsaw ($600)
- ❏ Bandsaw, benchtop*** ($200)
- ❏ Drill press, floor model ($400)
- ❏ Belt/disc sander, 4" ($250)
- ❏ Jointer ($400)
- ❏ Air tool set ($100)
- ❏ Drill/driver, cordless ($140)

Subtotal: $2,940

STAGE IV TOOLS

- ❏ Radial-arm saw, stationary ($450)
- ❏ Bandsaw, stationary ($500)
- ❏ Thickness planer ($450)
- ❏ Router/shaper ($250)
- ❏ Wood lathe ($300)
- ❏ Arc welder ($350)
- ❏ Grinder, rotary ($140)
- ❏ Power drill, ½" ($175)

Subtotal: $2,615

TOTAL: $7,765

SHOP ACCESSORY AND SUPPLY
BUYING GUIDE

The chart below recaps suggested accessories and supplies for each of the sample workshops suggested on the previous pages. Check off the equipment you find appropriate for your workshop. As with the Shop Tool Buying Guide, mix and match them to your needs. Also note that these groups of accessories and supplies accumulate for the successively complex workshops. For example, if you aim for the Woodworker Workshop, consider accessories listed for the Start-Up, the Homeowner, as well as the Woodworker Workshop. The prices given are intended as a rough guide to help you in your planning; adjust as necessary.

THE START-UP WORKSHOP—Total Budget $725
❑ Eye and ear protection ($25) ❑ Workbench ($50) ❑ Toolbox or bucket ($30) ❑ Machinist's vise ($25) ❑ Sawhorse brackets ($20) ❑ Router bits ($50) ❑ Handsaw, rip ($15) ❑ Handsaw, crosscut ($15) ❑ Hacksaw ($10) ❑ Coping saw ($10) ❑ Screwdriver set ($25) ❑ Pliers set ($20) ❑ Diagonal cutters ($6) ❑ Adjustable wrench, Crescent ($10) ❑ Open-end wrenches, reg. ($30) ❑ Open-end wrenches, metric ($30) ❑ Socket set ($50) ❑ Measuring tape ($10) ❑ Steel square ($8) ❑ Hammer ($15) ❑ Nail sets ($4) ❑ Awl ($4) ❑ Level, 24″ ($25) ❑ Level, torpedo ($10) ❑ Block plane ($10) ❑ C-clamps, four ($25) ❑ Pipe clamps, four ($40) ❑ Multi-meter tester ($20) ❑ Soldering gun ($20) ❑ Putty knife, 1″ ($2) ❑ Broad knife, 6″ ($6) ❑ Utility knife ($5) ❑ Paint scraper ($5) ❑ Extension cord ($10) ❑ Other supplies ($85).

THE HOMEOWNER WORKSHOP—Total Budget $745
❑ Workbench, extra ($50) ❑ Toolboxes or totes, two extra ($40) ❑ Ladder, 5′ step ($30) ❑ Ladder, extension ($75) ❑ Router bits, additional ($75) ❑ Drill bits, additional ($35) ❑ Saw blades, additional ($75) ❑ Extension cords, two extra ($20) ❑ Drop light ($10) ❑ Glass cutter ($5) ❑ Sharpening stones ($25) ❑ Cold chisels ($20) ❑ Deep sockets, ¼″ ($20) ❑ Tin snips ($10) ❑ Caulking gun ($5) ❑ Basin wrench ($10) ❑ Magnifier headset ($15) ❑ Face shield ($15) ❑ Combination square ($10) ❑ Wire brush, hand ($5) ❑ Spring clamps, four ($15) ❑ Tack hammer, magnetic ($5) ❑ Leather punch ($30) ❑ Wire connector set, solderless ($15) ❑ Hot-melt glue gun ($15) ❑ Other supplies ($115).

THE WOODWORKER WORKSHOP—Total Budget $1,400
❑ Toolboxes, additional ($50) ❑ Tool storage cabinet ($140) ❑ Router accessories ($75) ❑ Saw blades, additional ($75) ❑ Wood countersink bits ($30) ❑ Grinder wheels, additional ($35) ❑ Sharpening stone set ($25) ❑ Multi-purpose adjustable vise ($50) ❑ Level, additional ($35) ❑ Bar clamps, additional ($100) ❑ Metal drill bit set ($75) ❑ Mechanic's socket set ($80) ❑ Allen wrench set ($10) ❑ Channel-lock-type pliers set ($10) ❑ File set ($50) ❑ Sledge hammers, two ($50) ❑ Ball peen hammers, two ($30) ❑ Battery charger ($40) ❑ Nail pullers ($50) ❑ Painting accessories, additional ($100) ❑ Respirator ($45) ❑ Electrical tools, additional ($60) ❑ Plumbing tools, additional ($75) ❑ Other supplies($110).

THE CRAFTSMAN WORKSHOP—Total Budget $2,815
❑ Woodworker's bench ($500) ❑ Wood vise ($125) ❑ Wood mallets, two ($35) ❑ Wooden clamps, four ($80) ❑ Bar clamps, four additional ($60) ❑ C-clamps, additional ($20) ❑ Try/miter square ($20) ❑ Dovetail square ($40) ❑ Marking gauge ($25) ❑ Sliding bevel ($15) ❑ Caliper, outside ($30) ❑ Divider ($15) ❑ Steel rule, precision ($10) ❑ Bench level ($75) ❑ Drawing tool kit ($65) ❑ Ripsaw, quality ($40) ❑ Crosscut saw, quality ($40) ❑ Dovetail saw ($20) ❑ Detailing saw ($15) ❑ Bench plane, short ($150) ❑ Bench plane, medium ($160) ❑ Chisel plane ($120) ❑ Trimming plane ($75) ❑ Spokeshave, convex ($55) ❑ Spokeshave, concave ($55) ❑ Drawknife ($40) ❑ Palm plane ($15) ❑ Brass plane ($30) ❑ Wood-rasp set ($125) ❑ Chisel set ($100) ❑ Carving tool set ($150) ❑ Turning tool set ($150) ❑ Circle cutter ($25) ❑ Forstner bits set ($125) ❑ Screwdriver set ($60) ❑ Other supplies ($150).

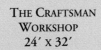

THE CRAFTSMAN
WORKSHOP
24′ x 32′

THE WOODWORKER
WORKSHOP
22′ x 24′

THE HOMEOWNER
WORKSHOP
14′ x 20′

THE START-UP
WORKSHOP
8′ x 12′

SCALE: 1″ = 6′

SUGGESTED WORKSHOP SPACE ALLOTMENTS

WORKSHOP	TYPE OF SPACE	AREA SUGGESTED	STORAGE METHOD
THE START-UP WORKSHOP	Basement Room or Garage End Wall	8′ x 12′ or 96 sq. ft.	Open Shelving
THE HOMEOWNER WORKSHOP	Basement Room or Single-Car Garage	14′ x 20′ or 280 sq. ft.	Open Shelving, Cabinets
THE WOODWORKER WORKSHOP	Large Basement Room or Two-Car Garage	22′ x 24′ or 528 sq. ft.	Open Shelving, Cabinets, and Under Bench
THE CRAFTSMAN WORKSHOP	Three-Car Garage or Separate Building	24′ x 32′ or 768 sq. ft.	Open Shelving, Cabinets, Under Bench, and Racks

(continued from page 129)
$14.95 in major book stores, on the Internet, or by writing the publisher (see the end of this article for address.)

When this colorful 192-page soft-cover book was published it helped unraveled many of the mysteries of setting up a home workshop. The book was designed to help even beginners with ideas and suggestions on how to arrange a workshop, how to buy and use tools, and even how to make jigs and devices that can provide critical help on typical shop projects.

For example, **The Home Workshop Planner** advises that no matter how you may have started to set up your workshop, there are many ways that you can make better use of the space you have available, make your tools and materials more convenient to use, and—above all—make the time that you spend on your projects more enjoyable.

The book points out that a big advantage in planning a workshop is that it doesn't have to look like or function like anyone else's. Flexibility is on your side. If it works for you, and if that's the way you want it, that is all that counts.

How To Get Started

A home workshop is a personal affair and, unlike a production shop set up to manufacture a product, your workshop should eventually be your own personal sanctuary. Use your own ideas and adapt other concepts to fit. Above all, make your workshop a place of your own and make it special.

The specifics of your dream workshop might be hazy to start with. For starters, it would have a good heating and cooling system so you can thumb your nose at the weather, have plenty of light, and best of all have a special little office where you can sketch, research, plan, or just relax and survey the tools you have collected over the years as you sip a good cup of coffee.

So how to begin? The first step is to decide where you can put your workshop: basement, spare room, garage, separate building. Keep in mind that if you keep most of the workshop's components portable, you can always rearrange them as you gain experience with projects, and also take the entire contents of the workshop along with you when you move.

Check the sample floor plans shown. They are excerpted from **The Home Workshop Planner, which offers several more floor plans, and** can be helpful in planning out your workshop on paper. First measure the outline of your available space, then sketch out a diagram of the space, noting doors, windows, plumb-

Starter Floor Plans For The Start-Up Workshop

Set in a dedicated 8′ by 12′ area, this minimal shop starts with a basic workbench that can serve as the cornerstone of future shop expansion. Shelves below the benchtop can be open or closed with cabinet doors, and can serve as a catch-all for portable power tools, various fasteners, as well as accessories such as a handsaw miter box. A 4′-high section of pegboard over the bench serves as home to frequently used hand tools. Tool holders for smaller items, such as various additional wrenches, screwdrivers, and pliers, can be built onto the bench itself, or can be made or purchased for attaching to the pegboard. Simple open shelves can be easily built above the pegboard, and on each side of the bench, for additional storage of tools, fasteners, tapes, sandpapers, finishes, books, or manuals.

Starter Floor Plan For The Homeowner Workshop

This shop provides maximum versatility within the 280 sq. ft. of space offered by a modest single-car garage, as shown, or altered to fit an available basement room. To the starter workbench it adds a second bench, plus an assembly bench. If the assembly bench is on casters, it can be easily pushed out of the way to allow vehicle parking. Both workbenches are arranged for easy access to the assembly bench. One workbench supports both a 1″ belt sander and a bench grinder, while the second workbench provides an inset for a power miter saw so its surface supports boards being cut. The benchtop tablesaw can be inset into the assembly bench; when not being used for sawing, the saw's blade can be lowered to create a fully clear assembly area. Shelves or shelf/cabinet combinations make full use of one corner, while pegs and/or shelf supports provide for narrow wood storage within easy reach of the large overhead door.

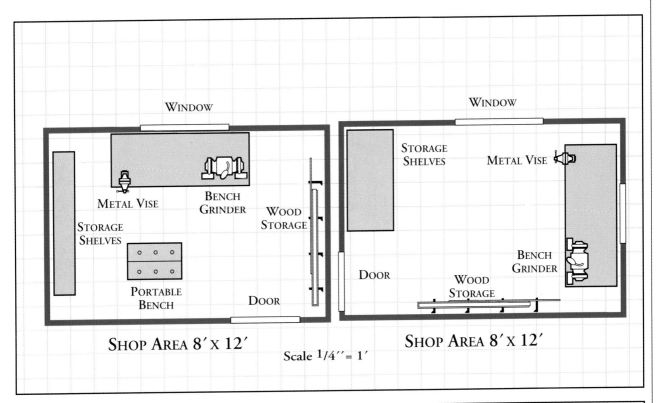

SHOP AREA 8′ X 12′

SHOP AREA 8′ X 12′

Scale 1/4″= 1′

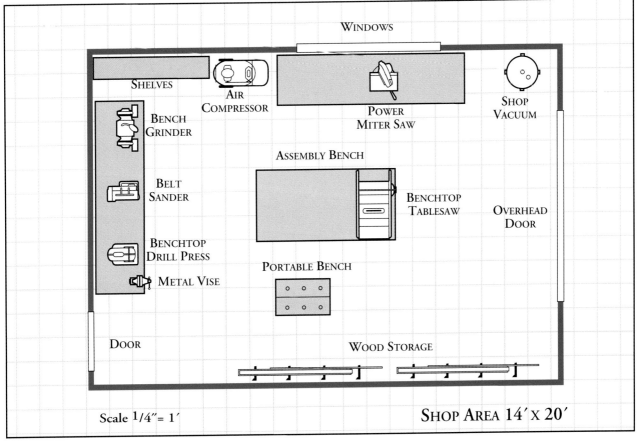

Scale 1/4″= 1′

SHOP AREA 14′ X 20′

When setting up your shop, carefully plan out workbench heights, which are generally made knuckle or hip pocket high.

plumbing lines, heating-cooling vents, electrical lines and receptacles, and lighting fixtures.

SHOP LAYOUT CONCEPTS

Your rough drawing may spark ideas for a basic arrangement. It may help you decide where to locate benches, cabinets, and lumber storage areas, and help you to think through shop working patterns in your mind. For any workshop it is a good idea to place main workbenches near any available windows to take advantage of natural light. When positioning major tools, try to have enough room around each tool to handle common project work and lumber lengths.

Also try to visualize shop work sequences as you decide where to position specific tools. You can use what designers call the "workstation concept." This line of thinking breaks down projects into subordinate tasks, such as cutting, sanding, and assembly, then grouping associated accessories and jigs for each of those tasks near designated major stationary shop tools.

The "working triangle" concept used by kitchen designers can also be useful in positioning tools, work surfaces, or storage cabinets to minimize steps during project work. The kitchen work triangle distance is figured between sink, range, and refrigerator, and the goal is to keep it under 26′. Keep this in mind, for example, when picturing yourself going from one major tool, to a second tool, and to your assembly bench.

After you have mapped out the top view of your workshop, you may also want to sketch rough elevations for each of the walls to help you decide how high to position the benches or cabinets. Note the ceiling height and sketch one wall at a time; doing this can also help you decide where to use pegboard, where to position other shelving, and where to locate electrical receptacles and lighting. (Most kitchen base cabinets are built to be 34½″ high without the countertop. Including a countertop with a 4″ backsplash and 2½″ of additional clearance, this means that 41″ is needed below windows and electrical outlets.)

OPENING UP SPACE

When measuring your workshop space, also doublecheck the squareness and plumb of all the walls. Whether the walls are slightly off may not be critical. However, if they are significantly out of whack, you may want to pre-build your benches or cabinets as separate units and install them so that any gaps along the wall will be less obvious.

Once you have decided on an arrangement, the next

Starter Floor Plan For The Woodworker Workshop

This shop, in space equivalent to a double-car garage, houses a full range of basic tools and provides adequate working room as well. It adds a third workbench and parts table to the two workbenches and assembly bench shown in the Homeowner Workshop floor plan. The assembly bench is surrounded by most of the equipment that would be needed while constructing or assembling a project. The assembly bench, the workbench opposite the assembly bench, and the parts table, are all kept at the same height as the surface of the tablesaw and jointer tables; this eliminates any need for outboard supports for stock being processed for projects. One workbench is outfitted with a machinist's vise, while the assembly bench is equipped with a woodworking vise. A roll-around cabinet housing hand tools can be kept near the open working area for easy access during large-scale assemblies. Wood that is stored along the wall can be protected from the elements and sawdust accumulation with a canvas drop front.

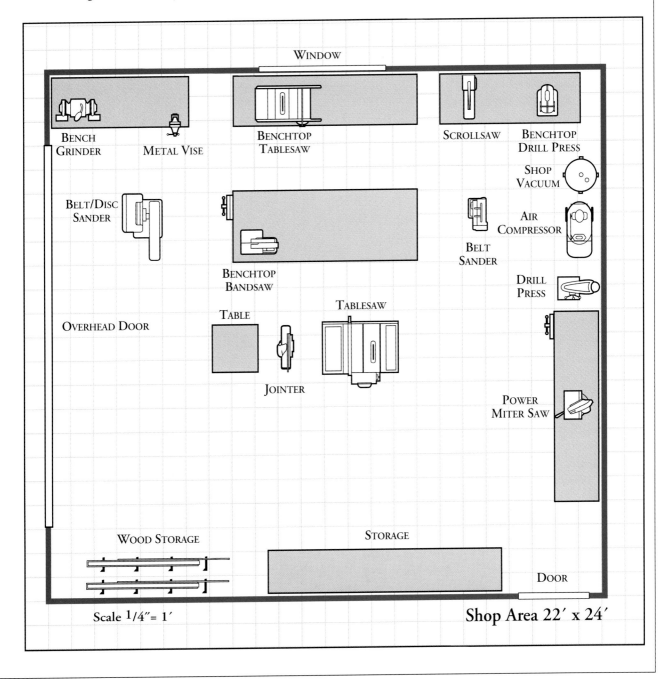

WINDOW

BENCH GRINDER

METAL VISE

BENCHTOP TABLESAW

SCROLLSAW

BENCHTOP DRILL PRESS

SHOP VACUUM

BELT/DISC SANDER

AIR COMPRESSOR

BELT SANDER

BENCHTOP BANDSAW

DRILL PRESS

OVERHEAD DOOR

TABLE

TABLESAW

JOINTER

POWER MITER SAW

WOOD STORAGE

STORAGE

DOOR

Scale 1/4"= 1'

Shop Area 22' x 24'

step is to clear out the area. That may mean creating storage space not for shop items, but for the materials that are now occupying the chosen shop space. For example, if you decide to clear a space in the basement, you will need to find a home for the stuff of everyday living that now occupies the space. Often redistributing home possessions to make room for a workshop requires using multiple approaches.

Before rearranging possessions, first sort through to find what you have. If possible, pick one large clearinghouse space where you can assemble items to sort and select those that should be tossed, recycled, sold at a garage sale, or given to charities. If you have lived in your home for any amount of time you may find that the search for storage space will need to extend to every available nook and cranny. You may need to leave some items in a pile until you have your shop up and running to build special shelves.

But sticking with your plans to sort out and reduce the storage load on your available space can pay off handsomely. It will not only help create room for your workshop but also, with fewer nonessential items using up valuable space, your home will actually feel larger, more organized, and more pleasant to live in.

EQUIPPING THE WORKSHOP

To help you formulate a general plan for accumulating workshop tools, review the Shop Tool Buying Guide on pages 130 and 131. Then, after deciding what level of workshop you would eventually like to have, skim through the Shop Accessory and Supply Buying Guide on page 132.

The buying suggestions shown are necessarily somewhat general to be of most help to most people. However, tools that head up the buying list for general woodworking include a good major shop saw, a drill press, and a router. Some shop owners start with a bandsaw or a radial-arm saw, but the tablesaw usually stands out as being the star of the home workshop.

Also, many shop owners find the wood lathe to be the most fun and rewarding tool they own. Priority hand tools include a few good hand planes and a good set of chisels. The key to using hand planes or chisels successfully is to keep them sharp.

Be aware that no two shop owners will likely agree on the order of tool purchases. The reason is that after acquiring a major shop saw and equipment to dress up lumber, like a surface planer and a jointer/planer, the tools you need will depend to a large degree on what kind of project you decide to build.

Starter Floor Plan For The Craftsman Workshop

Using a three-car garage or separate building, this workshop provides full woodworking, as well as some metalworking, capability. It is designed to provide efficient flow of materials. From the storage area wood can be moved directly to the radial-arm saw for rough cutting. Then surfaces and edges can be processed through the jointer nearby, and next run through the thickness planer. Besides an assembly bench, there are three worktables; two for wood and one for metal. One table for wood is kept handy to the jointer and planer, and the other near the tablesaw. One or both of the tables could be replaced with wheeled carts for transporting wood and projects. For convenience in parts fitting and assembly work, both the benchtop tablesaw and the power miter saw have an assembly table close by. The welders, drill press, and bench grinder are near the metal-topped worktable, and the rolling cart for hand tools is handy to the metalworking area. Wood is stored in the corner opposite the metalworking area. For greater safety the metalworking corner of the workshop can be partitioned off with stud walls covered by thin-gauge steel panels. If metalworking is not done, extra space in one corner could be used for a drafting center or office.

A GOOD WAY TO GET STARTED

The Home Workshop Planner book is a valuable resource that can guide you in all the details of setting up your own dream workshop. Besides showing how to plan your shop, it also has sections on how to set it up, equip it with the right tools, and how to use it to turn out your favorite workshop projects.

Each section is loaded with handy tips and advice, including how to build benches and tables, how to make your own shop accessories, how to organize and store your tools, how to build handy jigs and devices, how to modify shop tools, and how to make those tools more efficient and safer to use.

The book also offers great advice from old-timers, including how to buy used tools, how to start a project out right, how to store lumber, and how to successfully finish wood. To get your copy, you can order it for $14.95, plus shipping and handling, from: Meredith Books, 1617 Locust, Des Moines, IA 50309-3400.

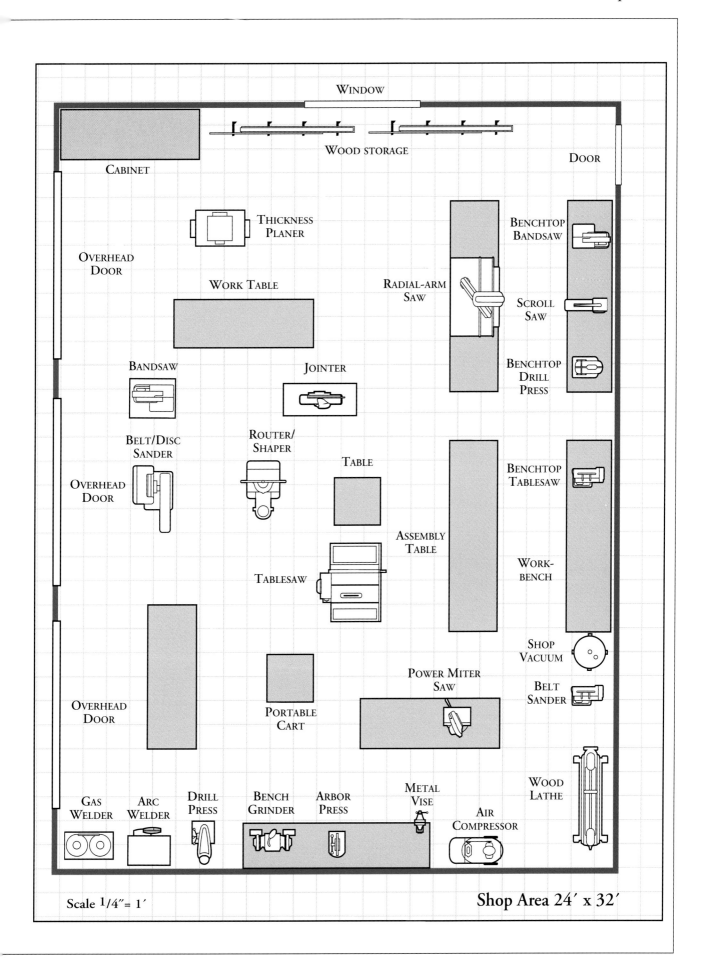

WINDOW

WOOD STORAGE

DOOR

CABINET

THICKNESS PLANER

OVERHEAD DOOR

WORK TABLE

RADIAL-ARM SAW

BENCHTOP BANDSAW

SCROLL SAW

BENCHTOP DRILL PRESS

BANDSAW

JOINTER

BELT/DISC SANDER

ROUTER/ SHAPER

TABLE

BENCHTOP TABLESAW

OVERHEAD DOOR

ASSEMBLY TABLE

WORK- BENCH

TABLESAW

SHOP VACUUM

POWER MITER SAW

BELT SANDER

OVERHEAD DOOR

PORTABLE CART

WOOD LATHE

METAL VISE

GAS WELDER

ARC WELDER

DRILL PRESS

BENCH GRINDER

ARBOR PRESS

AIR COMPRESSOR

Scale ¹/₄″= 1′

Shop Area 24′ x 32′

WORKSHOP TOOL RECORDS

Use these pages to keep a record of your workshop equipment inventory. Space is provided to list your tools as you accumulate them. Whenever the list is updated, make two photocopies; place one copy with your tool manuals, and keep the other copy with your household records. Maintaining a listing of your shop tools can pay off several ways.

First, you will have a complete record of all the tools in your shop which eventually could value several thousands of dollars. In case of loss, your records could prove valuable in making a claim. Second, at a glance you will be able to see how long each tool has been in service, the model number, dealer, warranty period, and original price. The listing will be handy when you need tool model numbers to buy parts and accessories, or when you are locating replacements. By filling in the tool service center section, you also will have a quick reference when you need repairs.

By keeping up the listings, you can also watch your tool collection grow and know at a glance its approximate value. The Home Workshop Planner book (see page 138) provides additional shop tool record pages.

TOOL	MODEL NO.	DATE	DEALER	WARRANTY	COST

Tool	Model No.	Date	Dealer	Warranty	Cost

TOOL REPAIR SERVICE CENTERS

Service Center	Brand	Address	Phone

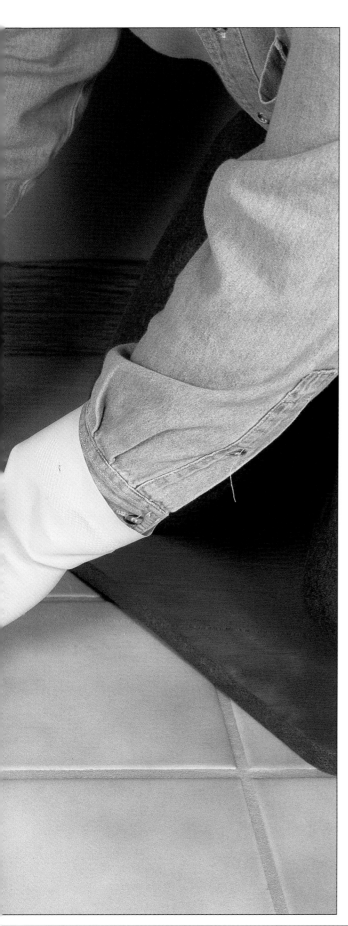

TILE REPAIR

A PHOTO GUIDE ON HOW TO
REPLACE DAMAGED TILE TO SAVE
BOTH YOUR MONEY & YOUR FLOOR

Glazed earthen tiles are one of the most attractive and durable floor coverings available today. When properly installed and maintained, floor tile can last a lifetime. But these tiles are not bullet proof. They will definitely chip and shatter if a sharp or heavy object is dropped on them. If this scenerio happens to describe your floor, don't despair.

REPAIR JOB OPTIONS

In many cases, if you have one or two tile that have been damaged you can simply replace the damaged tile and leave the rest of the floor intact. A seamless replacement really depends on two things: finding a matching tile and finding a grout color that matches the existing grout. With these materials in hand, the rest is pretty basic and straight forward.

In some cases, the installer may have left a few tiles behind for just such an occasion. If that is not the case, you will need to shop around. Check your local home centers for common tiles and also local flooring outlets for colors and styles that are less common.

If you are the original owner of your home, you may be able to check your building contract for material specifications. Also check for the name of the installer, who may have leftover pieces on hand. You also may be able to buy a few tiles directly from the manufacturer. If not, the manufacturer may be able to suggest a local distributor with odd lots of discontinued tiles.

If you can't find an exact replacement grout, by order number, visit several well-stocked flooring outlets. These often carry sample chips that you can check out and compare with your existing grout. Getting close

Two critical factors in replacing damaged floor tile are getting matching replacement tile and matching grout color.

1

To weaken the damaged tile for removal, drill holes diagonally across it using a hammer drill fitted with a masonry bit.

may not be perfect, but it beats replacing the entire floor. In addition to the tile and grout, you will need a small bag of thin-set mortar. Both the thin-set mortar and the grout will come dry, to be mixed with water.

REMOVING DAMAGED TILE

In the project shown on these pages, an 8″ glazed tile had a wrench dropped on it near one corner. The damage was limited to that tile, but the 3″ corner crack was fairly conspicuous. Luckily, both the tile and the grout combination in the floor were fairly common and were readily available.

When removing a damaged tile, there are two common pitfalls you will need to avoid. First, to keep from damaging the neighboring tiles, avoid prying against them with your removal tools. Secondly, avoid cracking the adjacent grout seams by using your removal tools carefully. Too much impact vibration can open up these neighboring seams. A tender touch and a little patience will pay off in a project like this, and keep you from turning a minor job into a major project.

To reduce the amount of hammer and chisel work, try to weaken the damaged tile so that it will break eas-ily. Begin by drilling a series of holes diagonally across the tile, using a masonry bit in a lightweight hammer drill. You will find that you can control the vibration of the drill by varying the amount of downward pressure that you apply.

If you don't have a hammer drill, you can try using a standard electric drill. A standard drill causes less vibration, but you can expect the job to take a lot longer with a regular drill. With either tool, however, a ⅛″ to ¼″ drill bit should do the job just fine.

FINISHING THE REMOVAL

After the holes have been drilled, use a medium-sized cold chisel to crack the tile along the line of the holes. Be careful, however. Glazed tile breaks like glass, so be sure to wear gloves and eye protection. Expect the tile to crack with very little pressure, so tap lightly. It is better to use more light taps than fewer heavy ones.

When you see a part of the tile loosen, tap that area once or twice to crack it into smaller pieces. Finally, use a small pry bar or your chisel to lift the pieces from the floor. Also use the pry bar or the chisel to scrape away the grout still clinging to neighboring tiles. Then

2

To complete the break, tap along the drilled holes with a cold chisel. Tap lightly until sections of tile begin popping up.

Use a pry bar or a chisel to pry under the remaining pieces. Try to avoid prying near any of the adjoining tile sections.

Lay in a quarter-inch mortar bed with a narrow drywall knife and shape it with a quarter-inch square-notched trowel.

Next, use a toothed chisel or a stiff scraper to shave out the remainder of the old mortar layer that still sticks to the floor.

Next, set the replacement tile into the thin-set mortar so its grooved undersurface crosses the ridges created by the trowel.

7

Settle the new tile into the mortar with a block tamped with a hammer handle. Check tile for level and uniform height.

8

Next, force the grout into tile joints using a stiff rubber float, sweeping across joints diagonally from several directions.

use a toothed chisel or a stiff scraper to grind the remaining mortar from the floor. Finish up by vacuuming all of the loose debris from the area.

Unlike wall tile, which are typically stuck in place with latex mastic, floor tile must be cemented to the floor with thin-setting mortar. To make sure you get the best adhesion, place the mortar with a ¼″ square-notched trowel. Flooring suppliers sell disposable trowels quite inexpensively. In any case, a square-notched trowel is a must, so don't try to improvise with something else.

USING THIN-SET MORTAR

Begin by mixing the mortar and water thoroughly, allowing time for complete absorption, according to the manufacturer's instructions. Lay in about a ¼″ bed of mortar with a 3″ drywall knife, making sure that the entire area is covered evenly. Next, shape the mortar with the notched trowel and lay the new tile into the mortar. Center the tile in the opening, adjusting the edges to match the surrounding tile, then tamp it in place with a block of wood and a hammer. Finally, recheck for both alignment and proper height and then let the mortar set the length of time specified in the instructions on the bag, at least overnight.

When the mortar has set completely, mix the grout powder with water in a small container. Both strength and color can be affected by the wrong amount of water, so try to follow the directions exactly. Again, let the mix stand a few minutes to complete the absorption process. Then stir the grout one more time and feed it into the tile joints with a rubber float.

FINISHING THE JOB

Sweep the float over each joint diagonally several times, until the gaps are filled to a level consistent with the surrounding grout. Skim over the surface a final time to remove most of the excess grout, then let the whole thing cure until the grout feels firm. This final skim won't be perfect. Expect it to leave a dry residue on the surface and some moist, heavier deposits along some of the tile edges.

To remove these remaining deposits, wipe the area with a damp absorbent towel. Then, in a few hours, buff the entire area with a dry towel. Try to keep from walking on the replacement tile for at least 24 hours.

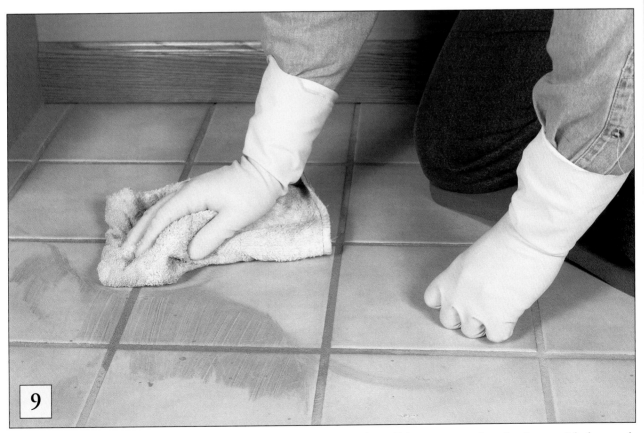

9

Allow the grout to stiffen, then wipe away excess with a damp towel. Buff the entire area in a few hours with dry towel.

BATHROOM OVERHAUL

How To Save Big Money
By Installing A New Bathtub
Or Shower Yourself

Nothing dresses up a bath like a new tub, partly because a new tub usually means a new tub wall and floor covering as well, but largely because it looks so substantial and fresh.

Tubs and showers built into the finished walls of bathrooms can seem unapproachable. However, these fixtures can be repaired, altered, and even replaced without the difficulty or high costs usually associated with such projects. Plumbers are paid well for bestowing this new look, simply because it is so labor intensive. And because "labor" is the magic word in do-it-yourself savings, tub replacement offers a chance to save big money. A job that would otherwise cost several thousand can cost you less than $500.

Old Tub Tear-Out. If your old tub is made of fiberglass, tearing it out will be easy. Just use a saber saw and cut it into manageable pieces. Few of us are so lucky, however. More of us are apt to contend with cast iron or steel.

Cast iron can be broken with a hammer, but the job is messy and potentially dangerous. As such, consider leaving that method to the pros. Instead, start by cutting at least 2′ of wallboard and tile from each wall above the tub. You will also need to remove a foot or so of wall from in front of the tub apron. If you hope to save the tile, pry it off carefully and stow it away until the finishing stages of the job.

These measurements are for the minimum amount of wall damage. For a more comfortable approach, consider taking out substantially more. In fact, if you intend to install a one-piece tub/shower, you will need to tear out everything to at least 6½′ from the floor.

First, use a drywall saw or a sabersaw to cut the

By tackling the job of replacing or installing a tub or shower, you can get by spending only $500, not thousands.

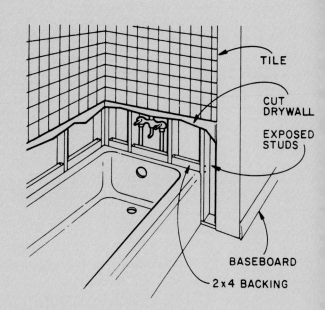

1 *When removing an old tub, clear out the drywall and tile at least two feet above the tub and remove the spout and spout nipple.*

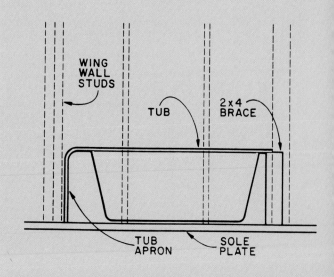

4 *When setting a bathtub, brace the back side of the tub with 2x4s. Before installing any wallboard, step around in the tub to see if it moves. If it does, use shims at one or both ends.*

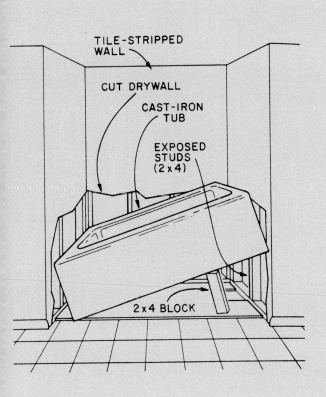

TILE-STRIPPED WALL

CUT DRYWALL

CAST-IRON TUB

EXPOSED STUDS (2 x 4)

2 x 4 BLOCK

2 *Lift the bathtub up a few inches at a time and block it each time. When one end is two to three feet off of the floor, stand the tub up.*

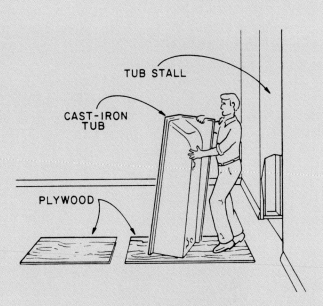

TUB STALL

CAST-IRON TUB

PLYWOOD

3 *Walk the bathtub out of the bathroom and house on two small sheets of plywood. Rock the tub from side to side, working it backwards.*

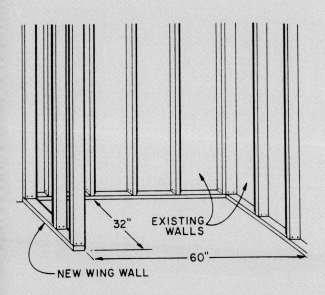

32"

EXISTING WALLS

60"

NEW WING WALL

5 *When installing a new tub on a long wall where a leg tub had been, build a wing wall for the valve and drain. The new opening should be 60" by 32" for a standard steel or cast-iron tub.*

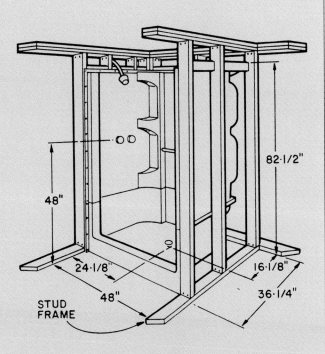

82·1/2"

48"

24·1/8"

16·1/8"

48"

36·1/4"

STUD FRAME

6 *When installing a whirlpool tub, build an elevated frame of treated lumber and finish in rot-resistant lumber. Be sure to leave an access panel near the circulation pump.*

perimeter so you can break the wall out in sections. Because you will want to replace it with drywall impervious to water, don't bother saving any old wallboard or drywall. If your bathroom is old enough to be finished in plaster, consider stripping the entire room and finishing it off with a water-resistant drywall.

With the wallboard cleared away, disconnect the waste-and-overflow drain and remove the tub spout and, perhaps, the valves. If your tub is made of steel, you may need to remove several screws from its raised lip, where it meets the back wall. You will then be able to lift the tub from one end and stand it upright. From that point, it is simply a matter of carrying it out.

If your tub is cast iron, the job will be much the same, only heavier. Because cast tubs have no raised fastening lip, they won't be secured to the back wall. Just undo the waste and overflow and have someone help you lift the tub a little at a time. Start with a flat prybar under one side. As you raise it a few inches, block it with scraps of lumber. Then pry again with a wrecking bar or a 2x4. You will be able to raise it inch by inch. When you have one end up about 2', have someone help you lift the tub into an upright position.

If you can, haul the upright tub out on a hand truck. If you don't have a hand truck, place several 2' x 4' sections of plywood on the floor and walk the tub out of the house on top of them. Just tip the tub toward you slightly, with its apron facing you. Then pivot the tub side to side and walk backwards with it. As you move off the first plywood sheet, have someone move that piece around behind you. By rotating the plywood, you will be able to move across finished floors without damaging them.

Oddly enough, this is a one-man job. Having another person on the tub just seems to confuse the pivoting motion necessary for a smooth "walk." As long as you keep the tub well balanced, you won't have to do any lifting. If you find yourself having to carry a tub down some stairs, get help. A cast-iron tub can weigh about 375 lbs. The best way to protect the stairs is to use a piece of old carpeting about 3' wide and 8' long. Lay the tub upside down on the carpet and tie the excess length up and over the end of the tub that will descend the stairs first. The final look will be of a bathtub riding down a stair on a bobsled.

To keep the tub from sliding too fast, position most of your help on the down side of the tub. Then, as added insurance, tie a rope to the tub's drain opening and have someone hold on tightly from above and let it down easily. To get a new cast-iron tub upstairs, leave it in the crate and carry it up with the aid of about three helpers. It won't be easy, but it won't be impossible either. It is less difficult than carrying a piano up a flight of stairs, and that is done all the time.

Choosing A Replacement. You will find a few more choices in tub selection than you would have a few years ago. Among them will be the traditional cast-iron, steel, and fiberglass tubs. But you will also see PVC and acrylic tubs. Of these, cast iron and acrylic are good choices. Cast iron is the most durable and acrylic runs a close second. Both are expensive.

The reason you might prefer acrylic over fiberglass is that it is vacuum formed from a single sheet of solid plastic. This gives it more strength, plus a shiny surface and solid color all the way through. Fiberglass tubs, on the other hand, are made in layers, have only a thin color coat, and are more likely to develop stress cracks. While fiberglass tubs have been greatly improved in recent years, they still can deteriorate with age.

Between steel and PVC plastic tubs, steel might be the better choice. While plastic tubs have been improved, they are still pliable enough so they flex when stepped on. Each tub will fit a specific need. Since cost is often a factor, you may choose a less-expensive tub.

Plastic and fiberglass tubs come in two forms. You can find most any model offered in several pieces or in one piece. One-piece tub/showers are bulky and nearly impossible to fit through finished doorways. For this reason they are more commonly used in new construction or in radical remodeling projects. The advantage of a one-piece is greater strength. If you have a one-piece in mind, measure carefully to be sure you can get it through your front door and into your bathroom.

Installing A New Tub. If your tub is made of anything other than cast iron, installation will be easy. All you will have to do is set it in place and connect the drain. For the sake of completeness, the following discussion assumes you have chosen a cast-iron model.

Start by bringing the tub into the bath. Remove the crate and set the tub upright toward one end of the tub opening. Lean it over until it comes to rest against the opposing stud wall. From that point, pry under the apron of the tub until it drops into place. Then push it tightly against the wall.

As a cast-iron tub cannot be fastened to anything, you will use the wallboard, and possibly sub-flooring, to hold it in place. Before you install the wallboard, however, step around in the tub to see if it moves. If it does, you will have to shim one or both ends. The best way to do this is to cut 2x4 braces and nail them verti-

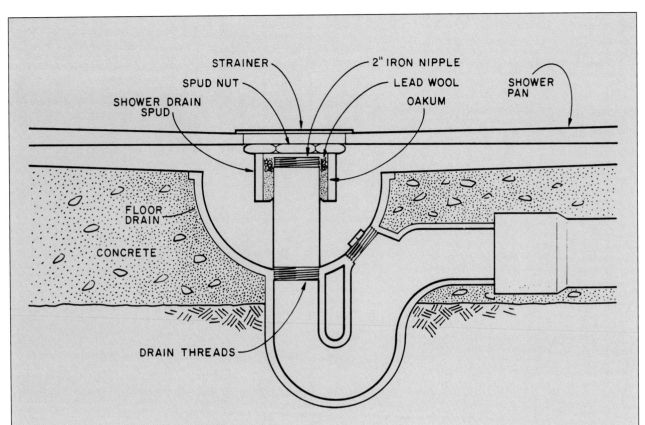

Cross-section of a shower drain installed with a lead wool and oakum joint sealing the drain-to-riser connection. The alternative is to use a rubber gasket. Oakum is less likely to work loose over the years.

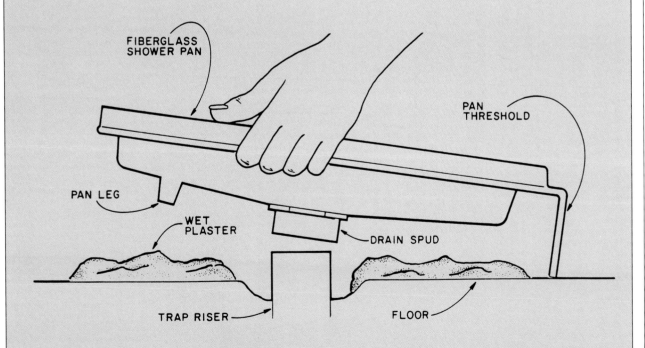

If you detect any movement in the shower pan, shim the support legs of the shower near the backside. For extra support, set the pan on an inch of wet plaster. Then walk around on the pan to secure it in place.

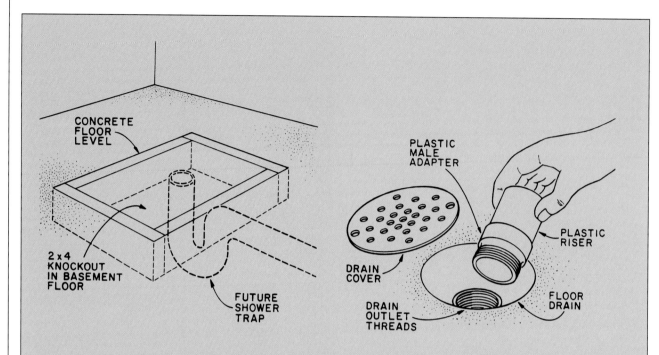

If your future basement bath has rough-ins for a stool and lav, but no shower or tub rough-in, tap on the floor with a hammer. The piping may be hidden in a wooden knockout box just below the surface.

Floor drains can be used as direct-connect shower drains. Thread a galvanized nipple (or plastic male adapter if the drain is angled) and stub into these threads for your shower-drain riser.

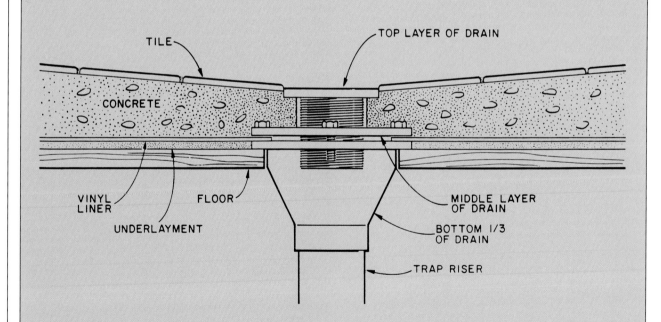

Cross-section of floor drain with a vinyl pan liner. Staple the corners against the stud wall. Clamp the liner in between the first two layers of a triple-layer floor drain, and pour concrete to the top of the strainer.

cally against the back wall studs. The back ledge of the tub can then rest on top of the cripples.

Replacing A Leg Tub. If you are replacing an old free-standing leg tub, you will have to build a precise opening to accept the new built-in tub. Begin by carrying the old tub out. If you have trouble getting it through doorways, turn it sideways and remove the legs. Then measure for your new tub wall locations. In most cases you will have to build one wall out a little, to close the distance required by the new tub. As for which wall to fur out, you will usually want to extend the plumbing wall.

If your tub does not set side by side with a stool or lav, but along a far wall, build a separate wing wall at least 32" wide. Place the plumbing in the wing wall. Whenever possible, keep the plumbing out of an exterior wall, especially in colder climates.

The exact length of a standard tub opening will be 60". Depending on the tub you buy, figure a width of 30" to 34". Then cut a new drain opening, roughly 8" by 12" in size, extending from the plumbing wall and centered 15" from the back wall.

Choosing Shower Stalls. The preconstructed showers come in three varieties and in several styles. You will find shower pans made of fiberglass and plastic. Because they aren't expected to hold as much as tubs, the material differences here are less important. If you install just a pan, you will have a choice between tiling the wall or installing a fiberglass or plastic wall surround. Tile offers a more traditional, and in some ways, richer appearance. But wall surrounds require less maintenance and are less likely to leak.

Next on the list is the built-in shower stall. These come in one piece or in several matching pieces. They are supported by stud walls and are finished against drywall. Many builders have gone to these built-in models to save the labor expense of tiled showers. Factory-made showers also shift the warranty responsibility to someone other than the builder.

Last on the list is the traditional free-standing shower. These showers are less expensive and are considered utility showers, best suited to basements, cabins, and work areas. Of these, consider the plastic models with metal corner supports. The cheapest are pretty flimsy, while the higher-priced ones are quite sturdy.

Build-It-Yourself Showers. A final choice in showers is the modern version of the original lead pan. These are built on-site and have as their only common features a tough vinyl sheet material and a layered floor drain. After these two materials are installed, the de-

sign choices will be varied. Traditionally these shower floors were finished in terrazzo, but today they are more likely to be finished in concrete and tile.

Because a home-built shower does not require a standard floor dimension, as with molded shower pans, they are more versatile. You can make yours any size. And, because they can be built with very little threshold, they are ideal for the physically handicapped.

Installing One-Piece Showers. One-piece shower units are the easiest to install. All you need to do is build a stall using standard framing methods. The enclosure you buy will come with framing instructions, but you can assume all dimensions to be exact.

The 34" x 36" shower, for example, will require a rough-in 36" wide. Since these plastic and fiberglass units have nailing flanges that you will drywall over, you will want to build the stall deeper to allow for a standard drywall corner bead. On a 34"-deep shower, you will want the stall framed at least 37" deep. If you are short of room, you might want to install a corner shower, which will require substantially less space.

For the drain opening in the floor, take your measurement from the base of the shower. Measure to the center of the opening and make the drain hole 6" in diameter. The extra area will accommodate the oversized drain spud and nut. Finally, bring a 2" plastic trap riser through the floor opening so that it is centered and flush with the floor.

Connecting The Drain. Most plastic and fiberglass shower bases do not come with drains installed. A drain may come with the pan, but you will have to install it. This facilitates easier packing and shipping.

Shower drains are installed just like a kitchen sink drain. Included will be a drain flange with a spud, washers, and a fastening nut. Turn the shower on its side to make the drain opening more accessible. Then press putty around the flange and insert it through the pan opening. Use a rubber washer, a friction washer, and the nut. Tighten the nut down until all visible putty is squeezed from between the flange and pan.

With the drain installed and the trap riser centered in the floor opening, slide the enclosure into the stall so that it is tipped toward you slightly. Then settle it back against the back wall. The trap riser should appear through the inside of the drain spud.

With the shower resting level and plumb in its stall, nail the nailing flange to the stall frame. The best nails to use are 1" galvanized roofing nails, primarily because they don't bend and will not rust. Place one nail every 12" to 14" along the nailing flange, but be careful to avoid hitting the raised edge of the shower wall. If you need to, place a piece of Masonite against the shower edge as a guard. When you have nailed the shower in place, and installed a valve and shower head rough-in, drywall over the nailing flange and finish the joint off with drywall compound.

When sealing the drain-to-riser connection, you will have two choices. You can make a traditional lead and oakum joint, using lead wool, or you can use a neoprene shower drain gasket. If you use a gasket, make sure you tamp it in solidly all the way around. Finally, snap the strainer over the drain and test your work with plenty of water.

Installing A Pan Only. In most respects installing a shower pan is like installing a one-piece shower enclosure. Because the pan will not be supported and reinforced by walls, however, you need to make sure the pan doesn't move around when it's used. Like a tub, a shower pan is locked in place by drywall, and sometimes, subflooring. The trouble you can expect is that these pans tend to rock in place slightly. The movement will be vertical, not lateral.

To test your pan, step around in it to see if you can detect any movement. If you detect a slight warp, or your floor is uneven, shim up the support legs of the shower near the backside. Use a cedar shim and glue it down with construction adhesive.

As an added precaution against future stress cracks, you can set the pan on a bed of wet perlited plaster. Just spread a bucket of wet plaster on the floor. Then set the pan in place, seal the drain connection, and walk around in the pan a little. Stay off of it until the plaster sets. When set, the plaster will give added support to the pan.

If you read or hear that you should screw the drywall flange of the pan to the stall frame, reconsider. Too often the screws break chunks out of the flange; you may be better off just letting the pan float a little. To avoid stress between the pan and its tile or plastic surround, make it a practice to hold the finished wall off of the pan about ⅛″. A silicone seam then allows the pan to flex without damaging the tile or surround.

Setting Pans On Concrete. If you intend to set a shower on a concrete floor, you will have one of three drain connection choices. Often homes are built with future bath rough-ins, which are intended to be finished by the homeowner. The shower drain rough-in will take one of two forms. Either it will consist of a capped riser pipe surrounded by a cardboard or Styrofoam spacer, or it will be an actual floor drain.

In some cases a builder will box out an area a foot or so around the riser and fill most of the box with sand. When he pours the concrete, he will then cap the sand with a thin layer of concrete. This serves to seal the floor against insects and rodents, and it also provides an easy knockout for the future homeowner. (Before setting a pan over the riser, seal the opening again with an inch or two of wet concrete.)

If you will be connecting directly to a roughed-in riser, the job will not differ substantially from that previously described. But if you must drain your shower through a floor drain, a slightly different tack is in order. Specifically, you will have to thread a 2″ nipple into the floor drain. These threads will be located at the very bottom of the basin and will likely be rusted badly. To prepare them for use, use a wire brush to strip the rust from the threads.

Then measure the depth of the drain basin relative to the depth of the shower pan's drain spud, and buy an appropriately-sized nipple. Thread the nipple into the drain threads using pipe dope and set the shower over the nipple. Then use a neoprene shower gasket—or lead and oakum—to make the seal. (If your floor drain was installed at a slight angle, thus resulting in a crooked riser, use a 2″ plastic male adapter and a plastic riser. Then glue the riser into the adapter at an angle opposing the cant of the floor drain.)

And, finally, if you don't want to mess with a direct connection, free-standing showers are available that have raised bases and exposed drain piping. With these, just run a 1½″ Schedule 40 pipe over to a nearby floor drain and dump it into the drain's basin. It is best to screw the drainpipe to the floor using a hole strap and anchors.

Building A Shower With Pan Liner. The traditional sheet lead used in site-built showers has been recently replaced by a tough vinyl plastic. This vinyl sheet material has all of the advantages of lead and none of the disadvantages. Most importantly, it weighs only a few pounds instead of a hundred or more.

These showers can be finished in a number of ways, but the liner and drain installation are pretty cut-and-dried. You will need enough liner to cover the floor of your shower, plus enough to fold up against the walls at least 6″. You will also need a plastic triple-layer floor drain. Start by cutting the drain into the floor and screwing it down. Then remove the second and third layers of the drain and lay the vinyl liner in place.

Wrap the liner up the side walls of the stall and staple it in place. Then fold each back corner into itself and staple the corners. All staples should be placed at least 5″ above the floor. With the back corners secured, feel around the center of the drain and cut the drain opening in the liner. Follow by fastening the second layer of the drain to the first layer, with the liner sandwiched in between. Most drains have four hex-head bolts as fasteners. Draw them down tightly.

Next, build a bulkhead for the threshold by nailing a 5″ board across the front of the stall. About 2″ back, and 2″ below the bulkhead, drill a ½″ hole in both side wall timbers. Then cut an appropriately-sized length of reinforcing rod and insert it into the holes. This re-bar will add extra strength to the threshold and provide a stop for the vinyl liner.

Then fold the front corners of the liner into the side walls and staple them there. This should leave the liner resting against the bar. To secure it, poke a few small holes in the top edge of the liner and wire it to the rebar. This should leave the top of the liner roughly 2″ below the top of the threshold.

Next, lay chicken wire on top of the liner and fold its front edge up and over the re-bar and back down to the floor. Staple the wire to the floor in several places along the threshold. Then cut a drain opening in the wire and thread the third layer of the drain in place. The top of the drain should be positioned 1″ below the back of the finished pan level.

Finally, nail a suspended 1″ bulkhead to the side walls to form the inner edge of the threshold. Then pour the pan and threshold full of concrete. This will give you a 4″-deep shower that slopes toward a drain height of 3″. The threshold will be 1″ higher than the pan and 5″ higher than the bathroom floor.

For the masonry pour, you can use a standard masonry mix or a special dry-pack concrete made for this purpose. The dry-pack mix will need only enough water to make it workable. Dry pack works easily and, because it is used so dry, you can form the inside of the threshold without using a bulkhead. If you decide to use a standard wet mix, mix it drier than normal, because the liner will not allow any of the water to seep away. And, of course, make your pour with the chicken wire suspended in the concrete as reinforcement.

After the concrete cures a few days, strip the bulkheads and tile the pan with floor tiles and a masonry tile adhesive. This masonry adhesive will not break down when wet, as will latex adhesive. When the pan is finished, install about 24″ of Durrock or a similar concrete board above the pan and continue with water-resistant drywall above that. Then finish with tile.

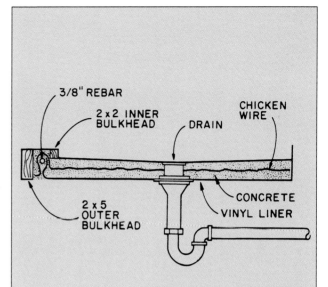

Cross-section of entire shower pan showing the position of the re-bar and chicken-wire reinforcement.

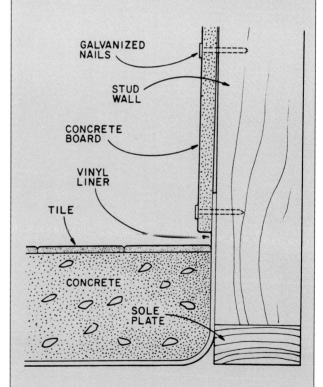

Cross-section at edge of pan liner showing how concrete board is nailed to stud wall to cover the turned-up edges of the liner. Finish with tile.

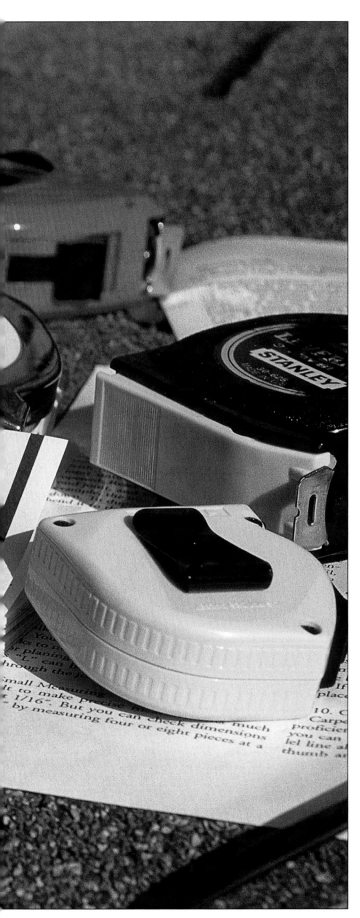

MEASURING TRICKS

HOW TO DO A BETTER JOB OF MEASURING ON PROJECTS LARGE OR SMALL

If you have problems in getting project parts to fit together, it may be time to sharpen up your measuring skills. The obvious problem with inaccurate measurements is wasting material. But often a bigger problem, if you are working on a large project like building a house, is having to re-measure and repeat a cut. If you need to cut boards twice, it will take you longer than someone else who works slower but cuts every board perfectly without any wasted lumber.

There are many tools available to help you increase your measuring precision. Which tools you use more often than others will depend on whether you are doing construction work or more delicate small woodworking projects. These tools will include the framing (or rafter) square, combination square, measuring (or long) tape, carpenter's metal rule tape, folding rule, straightedge, T-bevel, calipers, dividers (or compass), depth gauge, and the marking gauge. Also, in the category of basic measuring tools, you could also include the level, line level, chalk line, and the plumb bob.

For most measuring carpenters use the framing square and a 25'-long metal tape. The square usually has one 16" leg and one 24" leg. These lengths make it easy to mark for studs in a wall at either 16" on center or 2' on center. Although most carpenters today still carry the framing square to the job, new versions called "speed squares," "rapid squares," or "quick squares" are providing stiff competition to the older standby. The triangular-shaped squares, made by a number of manufacturers, have sides about 6" long. They are especial-

Using accurate measuring tools, taking accurate measurements, and then following through by making precise cuts are all essential keys to achieving a well-built project.

Most steel tapes today have a notch in the adjustable end for marking, as well as a slot that can be hooked onto a nail.

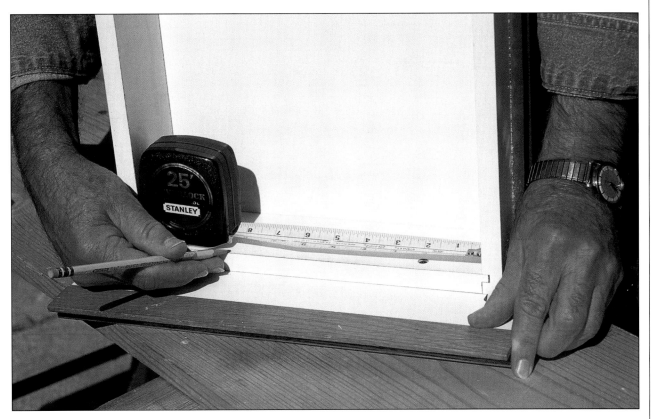

Steel tapes usually have the length of the case stamped on the side, which is helpful when making inside measurements.

ly handy for measuring angles and also can work as a saw guide when making 45° and 90° saw cuts.

The 25′ metal tape has a home on the tool belt of most carpenters. Because they are typically 1″ wide, they are rigid enough to make measuring easy for one person without any help. One thing all metal tapes have in common is that they have a sliding hook on the end which serves an important purpose.

If you are measuring a board and slide the hook over the end, the hook slides out to the proper position. If you are taking an inside measurement, and are pushing the tape against a surface, the hook adjusts inward to allow for its own thickness. Most metal tape cases are of a specific length, which is often stamped on the case. Knowing this length (usually 2″ or 3″) helps you take inside measurements. Simply set the case inside the area, pull the tape out full length, then add the length of the case.

Professional carpenters try to avoid what they call the "growing pattern syndrome." This is when you cut one stud or other piece to length, then use that cut piece to mark the next piece to be cut. After two or three generations of cuts, the length can be quite a bit off. If each stud, for example, is off ¹⁄₁₆″, by the time you cut four studs you will be off by ¼″. It's best to use just one pattern and use it for marking every cut.

You have heard the old adage, "Measure twice and cut once." Carpenters today usually don't actually measure twice, but they generally try to read the measurement they take twice as a matter of course—usually to ¹⁄₃₂nd of an inch. They mark the cut line, then cut just so the saw kerf is on the outside of the line. If you are not careful how close you cut to the line, lengths can be off because of the saw kerf.

One thing to keep in mind with metal measuring tapes is that their accuracy isn't always certain. For example, if the hook end of a tape gets bent, it can throw off the measurement as much as ¹⁄₁₆″. That can be enough to throw things out of kilter if you are doing precision work. Following are more tricks on using measuring tools for your projects.

Finding Equal Parts. A rule can be used to quickly divide a board into equal parts. If you want to divide the board into three parts, lay the measuring tool on the board, with the start of the scale against one edge. Then angle the rule so you get to a number which is easily divided by three (9, for example). Then mark the board at 3″ and 6″. By making those two cuts, you will have three equal parts. Likewise, if you want four equal parts, angle the rule to numbers like 8, 12, or

To divide a board into equal parts, set the scale of the tape to a number divisible by the number of parts that you want.

A metal tape's end will adjust for its own thickness. For inside measurements it slides in to keep the scale accurate.

16. If you want five parts, you would use numbers such as 10, 15, 20, etc.

Circular Widths. If you need to get an accurate measurement of the width of a cylindrical object, such as a dowel, pipe, or rod, there is an easy way to do it with a combination square or try square. First set the head of the combination square directly in line with one of the inch marks. Turn it upside down and slide the circular part up to the head on top of the bottom side of the rule. Next use another combination square or a try square upside down and slide the head up against the other side of the object. Reading the scale directly below the edge of the head will then give you the width of the round object.

Another way to find the width, though somewhat less precise, is to find or make two blocks of scrapwood that are slightly higher than the height of what you want to measure. Slide one block next to each side of the object. Then simply measure the distance from the inside edge of one block to the inside edge of the other. You can use a rule, square, or tape.

Remembering Angles. A zig-zag rule can be used to help you remember an angle if you don't have a protractor. First bend the rule at the first joint to the shape of the angle. Then, with the rule open about 3´,

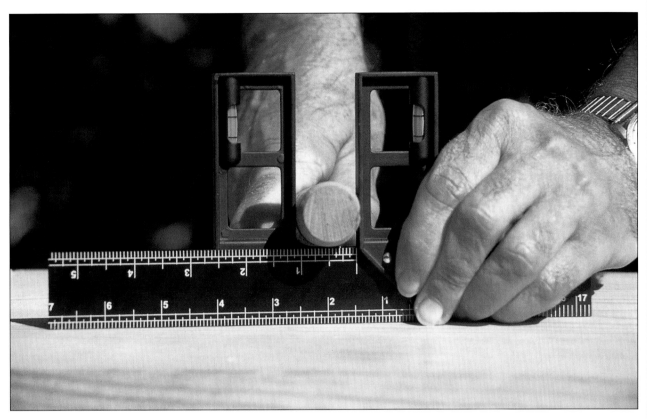

Either a combination square or try square can be used to find out the diameter of a round object by using this method.

bend it at the second joint until the tip of the rule touches the rule that is opened. Read the numbers at the first bend, the second joint, and where the tip of the rule touches. For example, the numbers might be 6-12-20. Write these down. To duplicate the angle, open the rule and just bend it to these numbers.

Dividing Boards In Half. There is an easy way to divide a board in equal parts. You can use a compass by putting the pivot at one end and drawing an arc. Do the same with the pivot at the other end. The middle of the board will be where the two arcs cross. You can do the same thing easier with a straightedge or square by drawing an "X" diagonally across from one set of opposite corners, then across from the other set of opposite corners. You can find the exact center of the board where the lines cross.

Using A Story Pole. You can use a piece of 1x2 or other narrow stock as a story pole for duplicating multiple measurements when constructing projects. Select a piece of 1x2 stock which is longer than the longest cut required for the project. Then carefully mark the height, width, depth, and length of the project parts on the 1x2. Use the measurements indicated in the construction or project plan, or use an actual part that has already been cut. By using this marked 1x2 for all

To find the exact center of any project piece, simply draw lines from diagonal corners; center is where the lines cross.

A tape can be used to check squareness by measuring diagonally from corners, whether a small drawer or large stud wall.

By drawing the carpenter's triangle onto boards to be processed or glued, you can later reassemble them in order.

of your measurements, each succeeding part will be cut to the right length.

Squaring With Tapes. Measuring tapes can help you keep components square in constructing projects. To determine if what you are building is square (when a framing square can't be used) is to measure diagonally from one corner to the opposite corner. This can be a wall frame or even a small drawer that is being clamped. Measure the distance from each pair of opposite corners. When the lengths are exactly the same, the project is square.

Carpenter's Triangle. If you are cutting a number of boards for a project, and have pre-fitted them together for a particular reason, here's a way to make sure that you will know how you had originally put them together. Simply draw out a triangle on the boards before making the cut. Some call this the "carpenter's triangle." Even if the boards get mixed up after cutting, you will still be able to determine their original position by reassembling the boards so the parts of the triangle match up when the boards are back together.

Close-Enough Measuring. Carpenters who do rough construction get very proficient at "close-enough" measuring. For example, you can use your fingers to help make a quick parallel line along a board. Hold the pen-

For ultra-accurate measurements, many carpenters and woodworkers will start at the one-inch mark on the tape's scale.

For rough carpentry, close-enough measurements can be made freehand parallel to the side of a workpiece to be ripped.

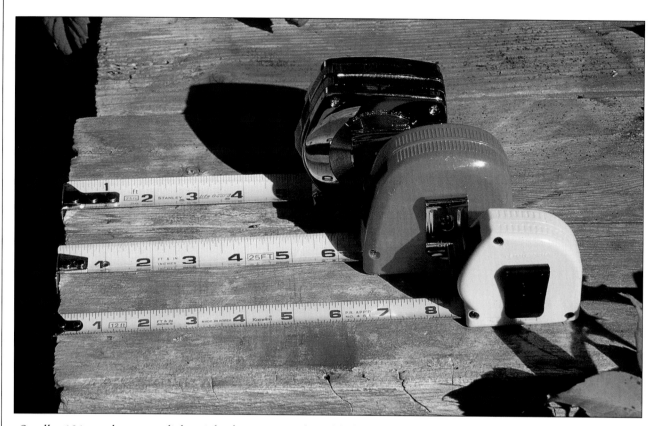

Smaller 12' metal tapes are lightweight, but 25' tapes have blades that will remain rigid for at least seven feet or more.

To doublecheck two metal tapes for accuracy, draw a line at a certain distance on a board and compare readings.

cil between your thumb and forefinger. How far you want the mark from the edge determines how far from the tip to hold the pencil. Brace the last three fingers against the edge to guide the pencil as you pull it toward you. A similar way to draw a quick parallel line is to place a pencil at the end of a combination square and move it along the board. Some combination squares have a hole on the blade for just this purpose.

Starting Beyond Zero. To increase measuring accuracy on any project, it can help to hold the rule you are using on edge to bring the scale closer to your workpiece. This is especially helpful when using thicker devices, such as the wooden zig-zag rules. To increase accuracy, some woodworkers will avoid using the zero end of a rule or tape and use the 1″ mark instead. You could also use other starting points, such as 2″ or 3″. However, when using this technique you must be sure to remember to subtract that number from the actual reading further down the rule.

Synchronizing Tapes. Measuring tapes don't lie, or do they? Let's say you are working with a partner on a project, with you doing the measuring using your tape measure and your partner doing the cutting using his tape measure. If the pieces you are cutting are continually off the mark, take time to check both of your tapes

To accurately measure small readings, assemble a number of pieces, take the reading and divide by the number of pieces.

against each other. Drawing both tapes out on a board will let you compare whether the tapes are measuring exactly the same. One of the tapes could have been slightly damaged so that it is reading 1/16" or so off. If a measuring tape is damaged, the best bet is to replace it.

Ultra-Small Measuring. It's difficult to make precise measurements much beyond about 1/16". But you can check dimensions down to 1/64" by measuring four or eight pieces at a time. Any error in each piece will then be multiplied, making it easy to see how much the "group" of boards is off. For example, if you measure four pieces, all of the same intended width, and find that all four are 1/4" too wide, then by dividing 1/4" by four, you will know each needs to be 1/16" narrower.

Accurate Cutting Lines. Unless you are doing rough carpentry work, where a carpenter's pencil suffices, use a well-sharpened pencil with hard lead to mark your lines. A blunt pencil, held vertical to the rule, will produce a line that is too far away from the edge. Use the pencil at about a 45° angle to make the line as close as possible to the the edge of the rule. For even greater precision, make the cutting marks with a utility knife that is fitted with a sharp blade. Keep in mind how you will cut to that line with the saw. Many carpenters will cut only to the center of the line.

To increase the accuracy of cut marks, use a utility knife. But make sure of the reading; you won't be able to erase it.

BOAT HANDLER

FLOATING BAIT BOX

BENT-WOOD NET

CAMP GALLEY BOX

CAMPFIRE ROCKER

ICE FISHING HAULER

SPORTSMAN'S PROJECTS

A HALF-DOZEN EASY PROJECTS TO HELP YOU ENJOY THE GREAT OUTDOORS

There is nothing as satisfying as making something useful in your home workshop that you can use while pursuing your favorite pastimes, whether it is fishing, camping, or just sitting around a campfire telling jokes and eating your favorite snack.

The projects on the following pages let you do just that. The best part is that, as you make any one of these projects, you can dream of those special moments when the sun is setting, the air is fresh, and you've just had a grand day being outdoors.

Most all of these fun projects can be made out of plywood, still one of the best options for low cost and durable materials. And most can be made with the simplest of tools: a circular saw, sabersaw, power drill, and other common hand tools. Chances are good you won't need to buy any more tools than you already have to build any of the six projects shown here.

When working with plywood, it pays to note that any power saw breaks through the wood (and potentially can cause splinters) on the side where the teeth of the blade emerge. With a power circular saw, for example, the blade emerges on the side that the base of the saw is sitting on.

As a result, your chances of getting a rough, splintered edge are greater on the side you have facing up when you are cutting. The solution is to lay out your patterns or cutting marks on the opposite side of the sheet that you want to show.

The exception, as noted elsewhere in this book, is when using a sabersaw. Because the blade can tend to wander some, it is sometimes better to lay out your cutting marks and do your sawing with the good side up. Just make sure the blade for plywood is new and sharp and you should have no problem.

BOAT HANDLER

It happens every year. After spending several months planning out the details of the family's summer vacation, some poor fisherman—with children and boat in tow—checks into a secluded campground, only to discover that the only way to get to the water is through a tight little woods path that won't allow passage of a full-size boat trailer.

Things would be much easier had the fisherman brought along a small boat cart like this one for transporting his craft through tight quarters or over rough terrain. This cart is suitable for hauling a wide range of boat types, including kayaks, canoes, rowing shells, drift boats, flat-bottom jon boats or any other craft with a maximum beam width of just less than 4′ (the width of a sheet of plywood).

The design is simple, and it allows the builder to customize the cart to suit the job; it can even be adapted as a general around-the-yard utility cart. The platform is constructed from a sheet of APA marine-grade plywood. For smaller boats, the minimum plywood thickness used should be ½″, and a ¾″-thick platform should be suitable for heavier craft.

When measuring for the width of the cart, sufficient space should be provided between the wheels to allow for the boat's beam width. Also, 2″ on the outboard side of each wheel should be allowed to house the metal-angle sections that will connect the wheel to the platform from underneath.

The cut-outs for the wheels not only need to be long and wide enough to accommodate both the wheels and tires, but also the two sides of each slot must be close enough together so that the axle of each wheel can be attached to the metal angle.

The wheels can be standard bicycle types, which are available at any bike shop. Two matching front wheels suitable for a 10-speed bike will support boats of up to about 150 lbs., but sturdier mountain-bike wheels may be necessary for heavier loads.

Caution: Unsealed bicycle wheel bearings will not last long after immersion in salt water. Sealed-bearing wheels are available, though, or caution could be used to keep the hub of the wheel out of the water.

This boat cart is built from one sheet of plywood, with slots cut to accommodate wheels and optional tie-down straps.

The wheels are attached to the underside of the platform via four 9″ to 12″-long metal angle sections—one on each side of each wheel. (One 36″-long piece of angle provided the four 9″ sections in the cart shown.) Building supply stores carry the aluminum or steel angles, along with the eight ¼″ x 1″ carriage bolts required to attach the angles to the underside of the plywood platform.

A hole is then drilled through the center of each angle section through which the axle protrudes, and is secured with the existing wheel-axle nuts. The four angle pieces are then bolted at each end to the underside of the platform with the carriage bolts, which are inserted through holes that have been marked and drilled into the plywood.

At this time, slots can be cut anywhere on the platform to accommodate adjustable straps used to secure the boat to the cart. These 1″-wide straps are available from boating supply stores or sporting goods shops. They can be inserted into the slots and routed through the gunnels or over the boat, depending on the type of craft and how it is positioned on the cart.

Adjustable straps are very efficient, and they allow for a wide variety of tie-down options. But if addition-

Wheels are attached to the underside of the wood platform using metal-angle sections fastened with carriage bolts.

Boats can be strapped to the cart at their balance point for easy transport to the water. Extra blocking can be added.

Slots for adjustable straps can be cut anywhere on the platform. Straps can go through gunnels or over the boat.

al bracing is needed, various methods include using shaped wood blocks covered with carpeting that are glued or screwed to the top of the cart platform.

At this point, the plywood can be covered with multiple coats of paint to ensure a long-lasting maintenance-free existence. A scrap of indoor-outdoor carpeting over the top of the platform will facilitate sliding the boat on and off, and it will also protect the portion of the boat resting on the cart.

Now the cart is ready to roll, and it is time to load the intended craft onto the platform. If the boat is already on a full-size trailer, it should be pulled part-way off the trailer before the cart is positioned under the hull near the boat's balance point. After the adjustable straps are secured, the hull can be balanced from one end, and the cart can be pushed or pulled to the water.

If the boat to be hauled is on the ground, one end of the hull should be lifted enough to allow for positioning of the cart at the balance point underneath. Then the straps can be secured, and the cart moved. For long, narrow lightweight hulls, such as those of rowing shells, it may be just as easy to attach the cart near one end of the hull and walk to the water supporting the other end of the boat.

If you want to use this idea for a general around-the-yard cart, attach a handle as shown on the next page and then add a carrying box on top of the platform between the wheels. The handle can be made of a dowel and plywood, with each side of the handle attached with bolts to cleats under the platform. You also could use metal tubing, bent to a similar shape, and attach it in a similar manner.

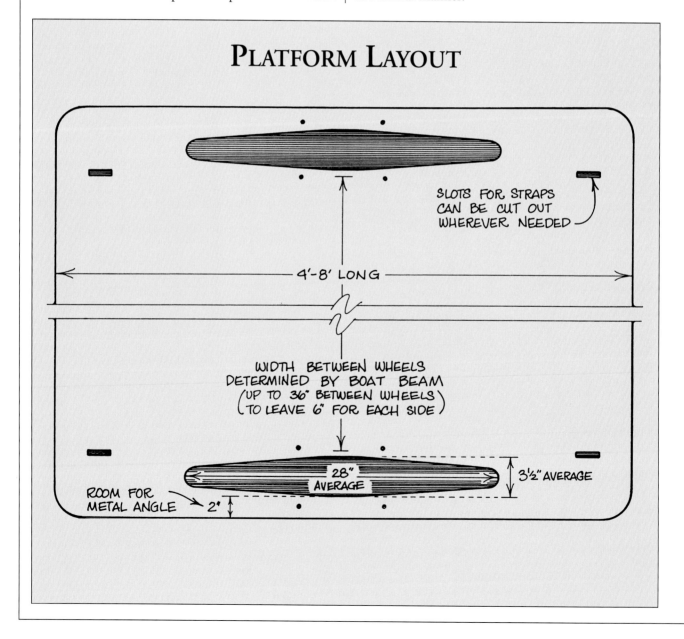

PLATFORM LAYOUT

SLOTS FOR STRAPS CAN BE CUT OUT WHEREVER NEEDED

4'-8' LONG

WIDTH BETWEEN WHEELS DETERMINED BY BOAT BEAM
(UP TO 36" BETWEEN WHEELS)
(TO LEAVE 6" FOR EACH SIDE)

28" AVERAGE

3½" AVERAGE

ROOM FOR METAL ANGLE → 2"

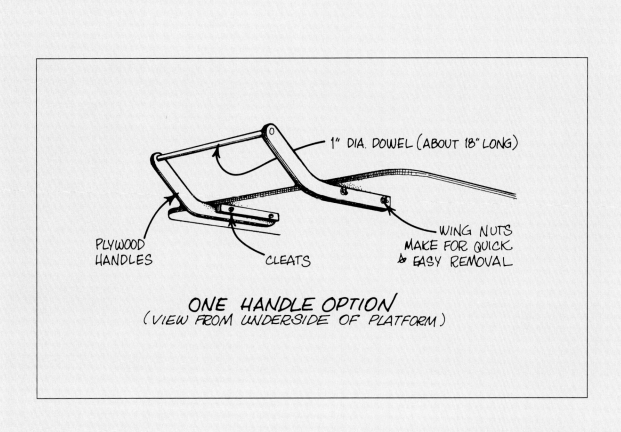

1" DIA. DOWEL (ABOUT 18" LONG)

WING NUTS
MAKE FOR QUICK
& EASY REMOVAL

PLYWOOD
HANDLES

CLEATS

ONE HANDLE OPTION
(VIEW FROM UNDERSIDE OF PLATFORM)

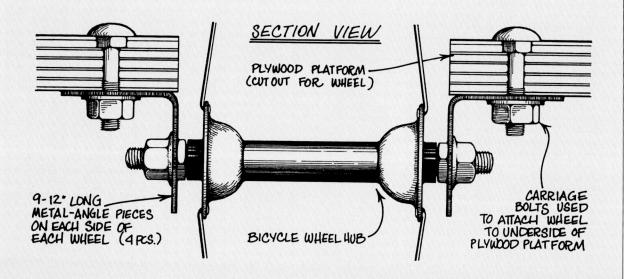

SECTION VIEW

PLYWOOD PLATFORM
(CUT OUT FOR WHEEL)

9-12" LONG
METAL-ANGLE PIECES
ON EACH SIDE OF
EACH WHEEL (4 PCS.)

BICYCLE WHEEL HUB

CARRIAGE
BOLTS USED
TO ATTACH WHEEL
TO UNDERSIDE OF
PLYWOOD PLATFORM

Two top access hinges on the floating bait box allow the angler to reach the entire interior of box with a dip net.

Grillwork at both of the ends allows for water circulation, while the top hatches help keep the bait shaded and cool.

FLOATING BAIT BOX

Fishing today can involve complicated electronics, expensive boats, and lures that do everything from glow in the dark to swim back to the boat on their own. But, despite these many so-called advances, a good number of anglers still enjoy the simplicity of the good old days.

Sure, they may now be equipped with rods and reels that are constructed more scientifically, and their fishing lines may now be able to withstand a bit more punishment. But what's at the end of those lines has remained unchanged through it all.

These are the live-bait anglers, and the baitfish that most of them place on their hooks not only still have the same appeal to big gamefish, but they also require the same careful handling and maintenance to keep them alive and swimming.

One of the most important pieces of equipment for this type of fisherman continues to be the live-bait box. The problem with most of those commercially available, however, is that they are designed for use in the boat or on the dock, where most times it's necessary to periodically change oxygen-depleted water to avoid having baitfish go belly-up. To combat the oxygen problem, commercial models have aerators as options, but most of the time the devices just serve to complicate matters.

Today's live-bait fisherman would do well to go back a few years to a simple bait box that was ingeniously designed not only to keep baitfish alive and easily accessible, but also to keep the gamefish taken during the day fresh and swimming—and in releasable condition should it later be decided to let them go.

The bait box shown is just such an item. It is a plywood container designed to float almost submerged alongside or behind a boat or from a dock. The box has two hinged access hatches in the top, while the front and back end openings have a grillwork to allow for thorough water circulation.

A top-hinged plywood flap on the angled front edge closes as the tank is towed through the water, preventing damage to both the baitfish and the day's catch.

When forward motion stops, this front flap opens as a result of the natural buoyancy of plywood.

The hinged lift-up hatches on top provide easy access to the tank's entire interior, and they are large enough to allow for the use of a dip net to scoop bait as needed. The cover also provides needed shade for the fish on hot days when the surface of the water is already warm. If you plan on keeping your catch alive, it would be worthwhile to install a screen partition inside the tank to prevent the larger fish from eating the bait.

The box should float with 2″ to 4″ of the top above the water to provide better cover for any fish inside. It may be necessary to place weight inside the box to make it float deeper. Temporary weights, such as small flat rocks, can be used. Or, small weights of any kind can be permanently attached to the inside bottom.

A towline may be attached to the front of the box by drilling a small-diameter hole in the tank, threading the towline through the hole, and tying a large stopper knot inside. There is a keel under the bottom of the box to promote straight-line towing.

The bait box is essentially a rectangular tank of ¼″ APA marine-grade plywood. The measurements are adjustable; the drawing shows one possible method for framing and building. Because there is no need to make any part of the box watertight, screws and small nails plus waterproof glue can be used to hold the sides, bottom, and top together. Also, although the box can be painted, it may be left natural, similar to the one shown, by using a clear finish such as varnish or polyurethane.

A materials list would include three pairs of hinges, screening or grillwork for the ends, 1″ x 1″ and 1″ x 4″ wood as required for cleats and fillers, 8′ of ⅛″ towline, a box of 1″ No. 8 Phillips wood screws and/or galvanized nails, nails or staples for attaching the screen or grillwork, waterproof glue, sandpaper, and a final finish as needed.

The tools needed would include a sabersaw, hammer, block plane, handsaw or power circular saw, small C-clamps, Phillips screwdriver, ¾″ Fortsner-style wood bit for finger holes in hatches, and a small drill bit for pilot holes to start the finger hole cuts.

The actual construction of the box is quite simple, basically involving measuring and cutting the pieces out of the plywood; cutting cleats and fillers as required; and fastening everything together. Any coarse edges are best sanded for safer handling.

The bait box can be built from one sheet of plywood; all dimensions can be altered to suit your materials and needs.

Bait Box Parts

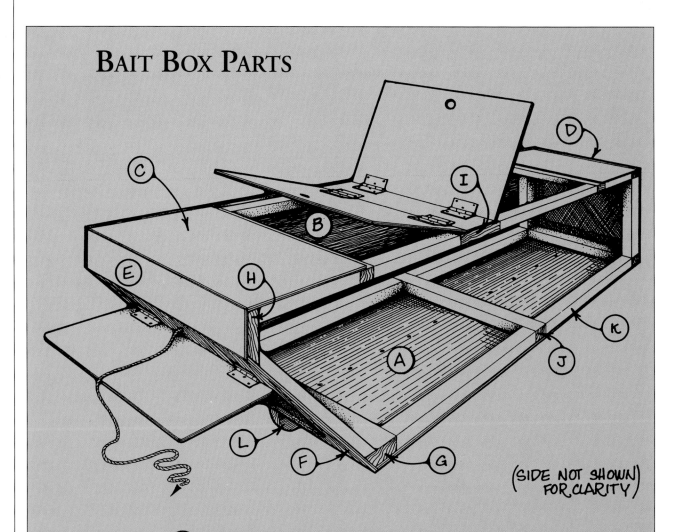

(SIDE NOT SHOWN FOR CLARITY)

- **A** BOTTOM · 1 PC. ¼" × 20" × 38"
- **B** SIDES · 2 PCS. ¼" × 12½" × 48½"
- **C** TOP · 1 PC. ¼" × 20" × 48" CUT INTO 5 SECTIONS
- **D** BACK · 1 PC. ¼" × 12½" × 20" WITH CUT OUT IN CENTER
- **E** FRONT · 1 PC. ¼" × 2½" × 20"
- **F** FRONT · 1 PC. ¼" × 14" × 20" WITH DOOR CUT OUT
- **G** CLEAT · 1 PC. 1" × 4" × 20" WITH ANGLE CUT
- **H** CLEAT · 1 PC. 1" × 4" × 20" WITH ANGLE CUT
- **I** HINGE CLEAT · 1 PC. 1" × 4" × 20"
- **J** CLEATS · 5 PCS. 1" × 1" × 20"
- **K** CLEATS · 16 PCS. 1" × 1" CUT TO LENGTH
- **L** KEEL · 1 PC. 1" × 3" × 38½"

The 45° angle of the box's front is important because it helps the box slide more easily through the water and it allows the front flap to float open when the box is at rest when it isn't being towed.

The front door can be cut from the same piece of plywood used to cover that end. Two small hinges are then attached to the top edge of this cutout, allowing it to swing open, and it is reattached to the end. The same procedure works for the back end, except that no door is required, and the plywood cutout is left open.

The grillwork or screening is simply stapled or nailed onto the cleats before the plywood covers are attached to the cleats. The keel structure is from a piece of 1x3 lumber, and it is attached to the bottom with screws or nails from the inside of the box. The cleats, or filler pieces, used to reinforce the inside and provide nailing surfaces, may be placed as needed. The two front filler pieces require a 45° angle.

After the bait box is assembled and finished, the only thing that remains is to load the box onto the bed of a pickup or inside a mini-van, drive to the favorite fishing spot, and plunk it into the water. Fill one side with baitfish, then spend the rest of day trying to fill the other side with fish for the frying pan.

The hinged door on the 45°-angled front closes during towing between fishing spots and opens when it floats still.

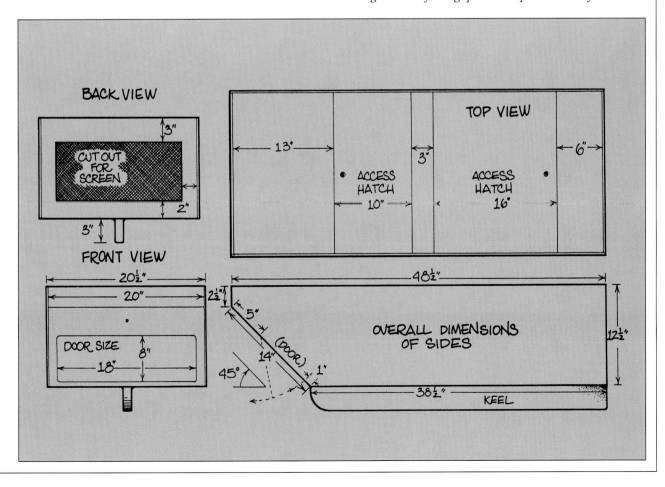

Two camp rockers can be built from one 4' x 8' sheet of APA plywood using the scaled patterns and the cutting layout.

CAMPFIRE ROCKER

This handy traveling rocker is easy enough to build so you can make one for every member of the family. It can be assembled and disassembled in seconds for convenient and easy transporting.

When taken apart, the rocker consists of four small pieces of plywood that fold flat for easy storage at home or on the road. Two hardwood wedges are used to keep the rocker sturdily together when assembled for outdoor activities.

Two rockers can be built from one 4′ x 8′ sheet of APA ¾″ Medium Density Overlay (MDO) plywood. The scaled patterns and cutting layout can be used to lay out the pieces full size on the sheet of plywood. (Note that the cutting layout is for a 4′ by 4′ sheet of plywood, and thus would be used twice on a 4′ x 8′ sheet of plywood.)

To begin the project, the back, bottom, and one side of the chair should be patterned and cut from the sheet. Then the first side should be used as a pattern for the second side to ensure that the two are identical. Pay particular attention to marking and cutting the rocking surface of each side piece. Taking care to achieve a fair and rounded bottom profile will help make the rocking action smooth.

The pieces can be cut with a sabersaw equipped with a fresh, sharp fine-toothed blade. It is also a good idea to change to a new sharp blade halfway through the project since overlay plywood tends to dull blades fairly quickly. To avoid chipping out small pieces of the overlay, do not force the blade. Also use a sharp drill bit when making pilot holes in the cut-outs.

It is important to note that the slots in the bottom piece for the wood wedges should be cut carefully for a snug fit. And, although the wedges should require a light tapping to put them securely in place, they should be easily removable without any pounding.

After all of the components have been cut out, use a sharp block plane to go around all the edges. Also cut a small bevel on each edge to prevent the overlay on the plywood from chipping. (A fine-toothed rasp or file works best to bevel the slots and corners.) Next, lightly sand the edges with #80-grit paper before filling and

The cutting layout shown for the rocker is for a 4′ x 4′ sheet of plywood. A sabersaw can be used to do the cutting.

ROCKER PARTS

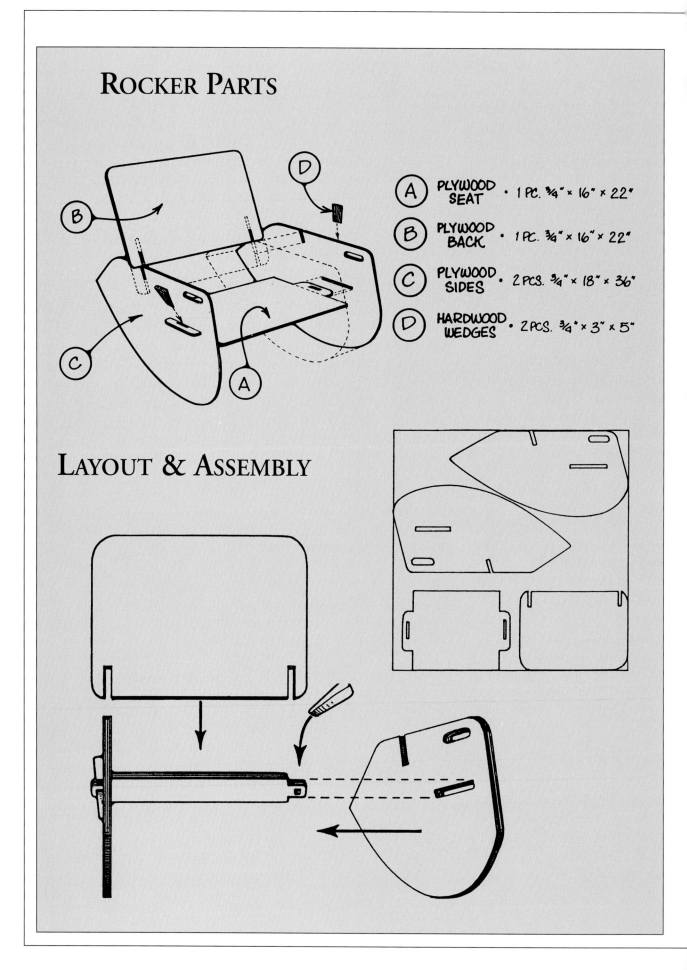

A	PLYWOOD SEAT	• 1 PC. ¾" × 16" × 22"
B	PLYWOOD BACK	• 1 PC. ¾" × 16" × 22"
C	PLYWOOD SIDES	• 2 PCS. ¾" × 18" × 36"
D	HARDWOOD WEDGES	• 2 PCS. ¾" × 3" × 5"

LAYOUT & ASSEMBLY

finishing the pieces. Seal all holes or voids in the plywood edges with wood filler. At least two coats of paint should be used on the edges; additional coats will help protect the wood even more.

The wedges can be of oak or mahogany, but Douglas fir can also work well. Each wedge is made from a block of ¾"-thick wood that is 3" long and 5" wide. A bandsaw makes quick work of sawing out the wedges, but a sharp block plane can also be used to work the block down to shape.

The taper should go from the full ¾" at the top to ⅜" at the bottom. All edges should then be given a slight bevel with the block plane to help prevent splitting at the top end when the wedge is driven in place.

A soak-coating of boiled linseed oil or Watco oil will toughen and protect the wedges from moisture. If the rocker will get a lot of use and be disassembled often, it may help to drill a small hole in a corner of each wedge for a lanyard to attach the wedge to the rocker to prevent loss.

A final touch, after the rocker is finished and assembled, is to add a cushion for added comfort. You can get some help to make your own cushion to fit, or you can buy one ready-made that will fit the seat.

A custom logo design or an initial can also be cut into the backrest piece to personalize your portable camp rocker.

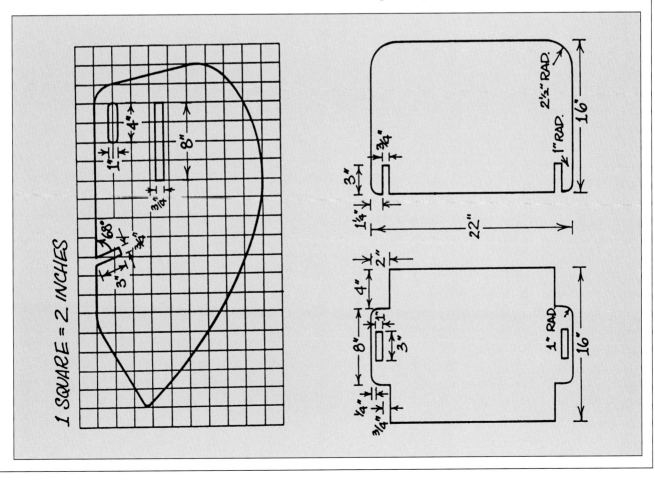

By using thin lamination strips and epoxy, this net frame can be made on a jig without soaking or steaming the wood.

BENT-WOOD FISH NET

This bent-wood landing net is made of wood strips, epoxy-laminated together and molded around a solid mahogany handle. The frame of the net can be made with a variety of woods ripped into thin strips on a tablesaw, and wrapped around a plywood clamping jig for gluing.

You can use contrasting woods, and you can even alternate strips of different colored woods for a two-tone effect. Domestic hardwoods such as ash, apple, maple, and cherry can be used to make inexpensive, yet excellent and unusual net frames.

The drawing on the next page shows one possible net shape and size. But the dimensions can be changed using the same construction technique. The frame can easily be made larger and stronger by increasing the size of the plywood form, or by using additional strips of wood. The net frame shown is about ½" thick with a total of eight lamination strips.

Wood strips used for this fish net were 1" wide and about ¹⁄₁₆" thick. They should be 6′ lengths, cut flush with the end of the handle after the epoxy hardens. After laminating, the frame of the net shown here was trimmed down to a width of ⅞" using a sharp block plane, a spokeshave, rasp, and sandpaper.

The best way to determine the maximum thickness for the strips is to cut a sample strip from the edge of a hardwood board, and bend it around the form and handle. Cut the strips with the grain. If they break or split, rip another slightly thinner and try again.

The strips should wrap around the plywood clamping jig and handle easily and without undue effort. Very small differences in the strip thickness will greatly affect bendability. When using epoxy there is no need to steam or soak the strips, which means that the net will be stronger and last longer.

Fasten the handle and 1″-thick plywood clamping jig to a flat board with screws to hold it in place. Cover the clamping jig and the board it is mounted onto with wax paper to keep the strips from sticking. Coat each strip with epoxy on both sides. When all are coat-

The completed net will be a conversation piece on fishing trips. It also can be used as a decoration on a wall or mantle.

After clamping of the net frame is complete, the laminated frame is shaped and sanded, then given a final finish.

ed, clamp them in place all at once around the handle and around the clamping form.

Space the clamps about 2″ apart, or as required. Begin at the top of the clamping jig and work toward the ends to achieve a smooth lamination. An extra pair of hands can be helpful since the epoxied strips can be slippery. Wear rubber gloves and use moderate clamping pressure to avoid squeezing all the epoxy out from between laminations.

It is best to use pads under the clamp heads to prevent marking the wood. Also, try to exert constant pressure along the full length of the frame. After the clamping is done, leave the frame overnight to cure at room temperature before removing the clamps. The next day carefully remove the frame from the jig.

If the epoxy sticks to the board in places, remove the attachment screws and carefully slip a handsaw under it to cut it loose. After the net frame is off the board, trim it to shape. A sharp block plane and spokeshave will come in handy, and a combination rasp will help with awkward areas. After all the shaping is done, finish the net frame with #60-grit sandpaper, followed up with #80 or #100 grit.

You will find that epoxy is a tenacious glue. It may

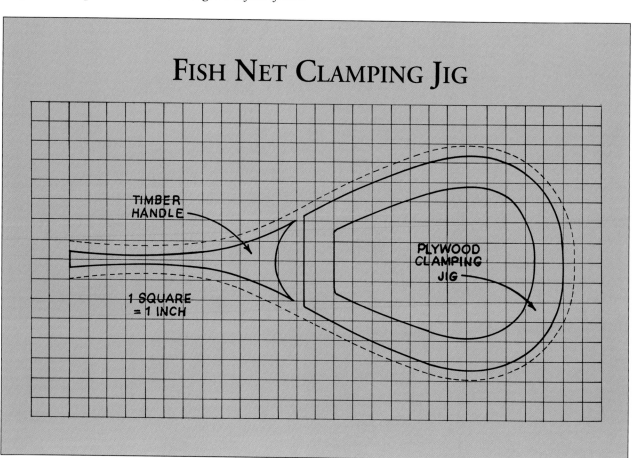

FISH NET CLAMPING JIG

TIMBER HANDLE

PLYWOOD CLAMPING JIG

1 SQUARE = 1 INCH

also be used as a surface coating to provide the best in waterproofing. You can cover the epoxy seal coating with exterior-type varathane for added protection from long-term exposure to sunlight.

The netting for the landing net can be bought from sporting-goods stores. However, it is not difficult to make your own netting if you have a net shuttle and basic instructions, which sometimes come with the shuttle. The net attaches to the frame by lacing it through a series of holes drilled in the middle of the frame, around the perimeter.

Be sure to have your net on hand, however, before you drill the holes in the frame. That way you will be able to make sure you get the proper spacing. There are various methods and knots for attaching the net, from simple to complicated. The only requirement is that the net be well-fastened.

A lanyard can be attached to the handle and equipped with a simple snap hook or French hook, as shown, for hooking the net to a belt or vest loop. If you are making the net as a gift, carving a name or initials in the handle is a nice personalized touch. Besides landing lunkers, the net can also be a charming wall hanging or mantle piece.

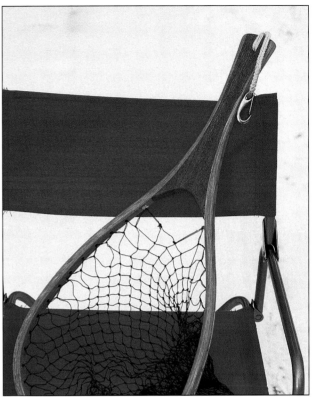

This lanyard is fitted with a French hook. Netting can be purchased, or you can make your own with a net shuttle.

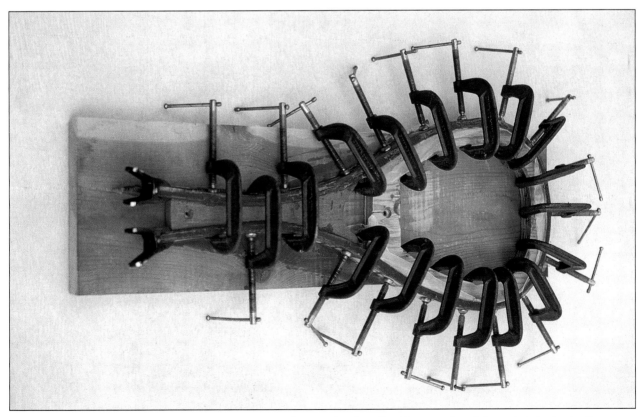

Wood strips are wrapped around the clamping jig and epoxied to handle. Netting is laced through holes in the frame.

With the lid open and the addition of a top tray, this galley box can be put to many uses, including a camp kitchen.

CAMP GALLEY BOX

This galley box is styled like the old military campaign chests that once held a soldier's personal gear. Made of plywood, it's ideal for car camping and will hold a variety of either camp and kitchen gear, such as lanterns, cook stoves, fuel, or utensils and food.

The small but sturdy box is animal- and insect-proof, and makes a fine seat around the campfire. It is built of ½"-thick marine plywood, and has ¾" x 3½" vertical grain fir molding wrapped around both the top and bottom for strength. The box can be assembled using 1" No. 8 screws and cabinet glue.

One easy way to build the box is to glue and screw the internal box together completely, then make a cut all around the box 3" down from the top before attaching moldings. The assembled box can be run through a tablesaw or cut with a sabersaw. This method will make sure the top is exactly the same size as the bottom of the box so it fits perfectly together when the molding is attached.

The top molding overlaps the sides of the box by ½" and makes a secure seal when closed. Use screws and glue and sliding clamps to fasten the box together. The first step in assembly is to attach ¾" x ¾" cleats (A) all around the bottom of the bottom piece (B). The cleats provide a gluing and fastening surface for screws inserted through the sides (C) and ends (D) of the box and through the bottom moldings (F and G).

Cut and attach the top piece of plywood (E) flush with the sides and ends so that it will fit against the top molding (F and G). After attaching the moldings, chamfer all sharp corners with sandpaper or a block plane. You may also want to cut an angle on the edge of the moldings.

The hinges need to be strong enough to support the lid, used as a cooking surface. The hinges should be held in place with large screws or small bolts. Depending on the type of hinges used, you may need to attach a wooden hinge support (H) to the backside to provide correct hinge alignment and to make the top lay flat.

The optional tray can be fitted into the inside of the box to help organize your gear. The tray can be made of ¼" plywood to rest on ¾" cleats screwed to the inside front and back of the box. The tray can then be slid from side to side and lifted out. The rope handles require only two small holes in each side and a knot on each end of the rope inside the box.

BOX PARTS

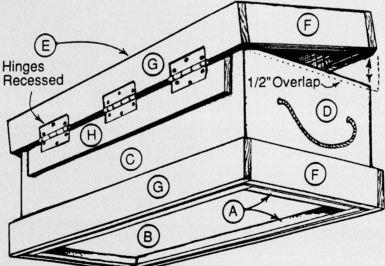

KEY: A. Fir Cleats, 4 pieces ¾" sq. x 7'6", cut to fit. B. Plywood Bottom, 1 piece ½" x 15" x 29". C. Plywood Front & Back, 2 pieces ½" x 14" x 30". D. Plywood Ends, 2 pieces ½" x 14" x 15". E. Plywood Top, 1 piece ½" x 16" x 30". F. Fir End Moldings, 4 pieces ¾" x 3½" x 16". G. Fir Front & Back Moldings, 4 pieces ¾" x 3½" x 31½". H. Fir Hinge Support, 1 piece ¾" x 3½" x 27".

ICE FISHING HAULER

Here is just the ticket to keeping ice fishing gear organized both at home and on the ice. Everything you need can be kept in the sled in storage, and it is all ready to go when you need it.

This ice fishing sled glides on runners made from a pair of used skis, which can be picked up for a few dollars at garage sales or thrift stores. Slightly wider downhill skis provide a degree more support in powdery snow, but even skinny cross-country skis can work, especially on hard-packed snow or ice.

The rest of the sled is built from materials that are available at local lumberyards and home-supply centers, and it can be assembled over a spare weekend. Following is a materials list for the sled:

One pair skis with bindings removed; two sheets ½"-thick APA ABX plywood; 18 linear feet of ¾" x 1" cedar or pine; 12 linear feet of 2x6 fir; one box of 100 1"-long self-tapping drywall screws; 16 pieces No. 10 2"-long Phillips-head wood screws; eight washers; two sections 1½"-wide continuous hinge for lids; one quart primer for bare plywood; one quart topcoat paint; ⅛" towline with optional PVC pipe spacers.

The gull-wing lid design allows easy access to any part of the sled. The hinge support board positioned across the center of the sled under the top provides needed structural support. All of the interior compartments may be arranged to suit your particular needs.

The interior arrangement shown has one full-length compartment to accommodate an ice auger, and smaller compartments for a bait bucket, tackle boxes, ice dippers, thermos, lanterns, stoves, rods, tip-ups, warm clothing, or other gear. There are two large handles on each side of the sled to lift it into a pickup truck bed or trailer. The handles also can be used as tie downs to secure necessary fishing gear, such as an ice shelter, on top of the sled.

The sled box of APA ½" ABX plywood is fastened together using 1" self-tapping drywall screws. The entire sled can be built from two sheets of plywood, which will allow left-over scrap pieces for interior dividers. The drywall screws can be inserted using a variable-speed drill with the appropriate bit. For best results use small pilot holes.

The ¾" x 1" corner cleats used to support the walls

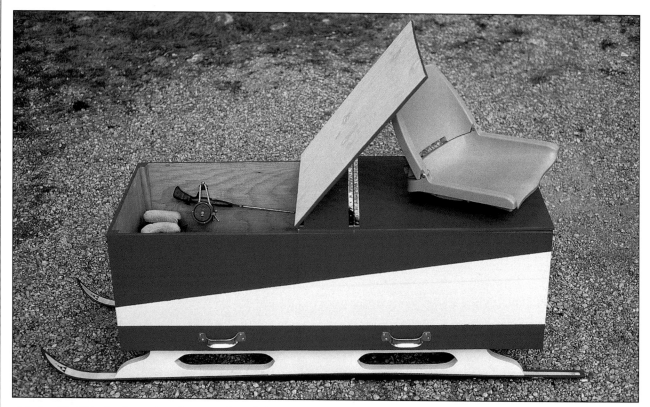

Made of half-inch plywood and a pair of used skis, this sled has space for an ice auger, plus all the other gear you need.

can be cedar, fir, or pine. All three of these woods are soft enough to work well using drywall screws.

The seat of the sled is a folding plastic model that can be purchased complete with swivel mounting hardware, and it can be bolted to either sled lid. These seats are normally used for rafts and drift boats and are available from sporting goods stores, boating supply shops, or by mail order.

To construct the sled, first cut out the bottom piece and attach the side and end structural support cleats flush with the edges on all sides. An easy way to attach the cleats is to position them in place with two small clamps, flip the plywood over and insert drywall screws through the bottom and into the cleat.

Next, the sides can be attached by clamping them to the cleats and inserting screws through the side. The corner cleats are then attached to the sides, and then the ends are fitted and fastened.

A 2x6 fir brace is fitted flush with the top of the sides across the middle of the box. This brace will provide a fastening surface for the top and will support the two lid hinges. The lids are cut oversize to provide a ⅛" lip all around for fingerholds.

Two 2x6 pieces of fir or pine, each 5′ long, are used to support and connect the skis to the bottom of the

sled box. The idea of the support is to force the bottom of the ski flat so it contacts the ice surface along its full length. Most modern skis are tapered in thickness, and the support must be scribed to fit the contour. To determine this, simply clamp the ski flat, and

KEY
A. Bottom, 1 piece ½" x 23" x 59".
B. Side Cleats, 2 pieces ¾" x 1" x 59".
C. End Cleats, 2 pieces ¾" x 1" x 21".
D. Sides. 2 pieces ½" x 18" x 59".
E. Corner Cleats, 4 pieces ¾" x 1" x 16¾".
F. Ends, 2 pieces ½" x 18" x 24".
G. Brace, 1 piece 2x6 x 23".
H. Top Center, 1 piece ½" x 7½" x 24¼".
I. Top Doors, 2 pieces ½" x 24¼" x 26⅜".
J. Supports, 2 pieces 2x6 x 60".
K. Skis. 1 pair, adult downhill or cross-country.
L. Drywall Screws, 1 box of 100 1" long.
M. Wood Screws w/washers, 8 No. 10 Phillips 2".
N. Wood Screws, 8 No. 10 Phillips 2".
O. Continuous Hinge, 2 pieces 1½" x 20" to 24".
P. Towline, ⅜" cut to desired lengths.
Q. Stiffeners, 2 pieces PVC pipe (optional).

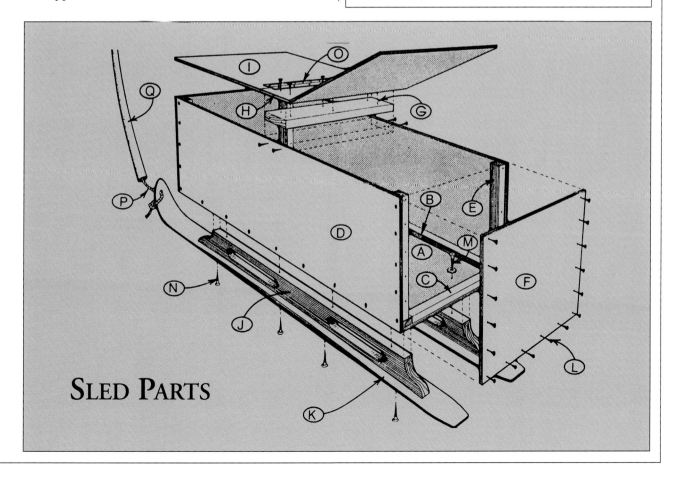

SLED PARTS

The two large handles on each side of the ice fishing sled allow easy lifting into either a pickup or a mini-van.

with a pencil, transfer the shape to the bottom of the support board. Cut the contour into the support board, and attach each one to a ski.

The skis are attached to the 2x6 supports using four 2"-long No. 10 Phillips-head wood screws for each ski. The screws are fastened up through the bottom of the ski into the wood support, and the predrilled holes should be countersunk to keep the screw head flush with the bottom of the ski.

Prefinishing the supports with a coat of paint or varnish before fastening them to the skis will save time later. The supports and skis are then attached to the sled box bottom from the inside of the box using 2"-long No. 10 Phillips-head screws with washers.

The towline is attached to the ends of the skis by drilling a ⅜" hole through each of the ski tips and tying a stopper knot in the line. If the sled is to be towed downhill by snowmobile or truck, it is a good idea to run the line through lengths of PVC pipe to keep the sled from running into the vehicle.

Brush on some primer, give the sled a custom paint job, and you will have a convenient way to organize and transport your fishing gear. The best part about building the sled is that you can keep that gear inside the sled in the garage or outbuilding year around.

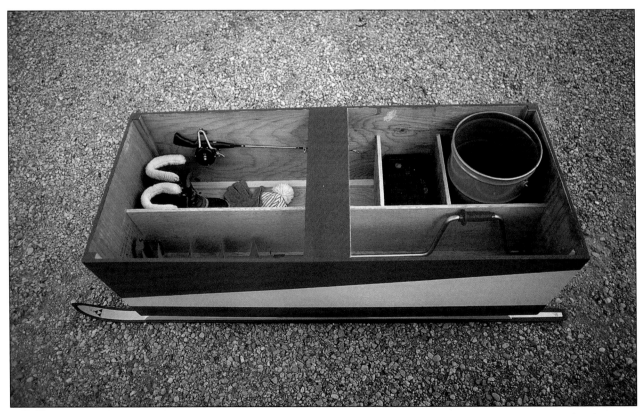

Nearly any kind of used adult skis can provide the runners for your ice fishing sled. A seat can be purchased at low cost.

INDEX

A
Accessories, workshop, 132
All-terrain cabin, 6
Angles, remembering, 162

B
Backfill, for retaining walls, 71
Ballast, for fluorescents, 107
Bathroom improvement, 150
Bathtub replacements, 152
Bent-wood fishing net, 182
Bicycle wheels, for cart, 170
Boat handler, 170
Boot grate, 18
Bubbles, in wallpaper, 112
Building
  bait box, 174
  boat cart, 170
  boot scraper, 18
  cabin, 6
  camp galley box, 186

camp rocker, 178
dog bed, 49
fishing net, 182
ice fishing sled, 188
kennel house, 46
picnic table, 78
shooting bench, 122
shower pan, 155
slotted shelves, 26
Buying, glues, 55
Buying guide, tools, 130
Brushes, for gluing, 57

C
Cabin, do-it-yourself, 6
Camp galley box, building, 186
Campfire rocker, building, 178
Canine cot, building, 49
Canoe/boat cart, 170
Caulking, techniques, 110
Chisels, glue removal, 62
Circular saw, using, 33
Circular widths, measuring, 162
Clamping, for gluing, 58
Cleaning oil spills, concrete, 120
Combination bits, 35
Continuity tester, using, 75
Concrete, driveway, 118
Corner bead repair, 20
Cracks, in driveway, 118

Curing, glues, 62
Curled shingles, 93
Curves
  laying out, 36
  in retaining walls, 72
Cutting lines, for saws, 167

D
Damage repair, walls, 20
Damaged tile repair, 142
Diagnosing switches, 74
Dimming switch, fluorescent, 100
Disposer, installation, 42
Dividing, boards, 163
Dowels, gluing, 62
Drains
  remote control, 38
  shower, 155
Driveway, maintenance, 118
Dryer vent, replacement, 94
Drywall compound, using, 24

E
Electrical cable, installing, 105
Epoxy supplies, source, 51
Equal parts, finding, 161
Expansion joints, fixing, 118

F
Faucet, installation, 42
Finishing
  plywood, 37
  shelves, 32
Fish tape, for wiring, 105
Fishing net, building, 182
Fixture sockets, checking, 77
Flashing, on roof, 88
Floating bait box, building, 174
Floor tile repair, 142
Fluorescent fixtures
  ballast, 107
  dimming switch, 100
  lamp sockets, 108
Fractional lengths, measuring, 167
Framing, hip roof, 10

G
Garden window, 12
Glues
  applying, 58
  brushes, 57
  buying, 55
  dowels, 62
  epoxies, 51
  storing, 57
  squeeze-out, 60
Gluing
  techniques, 52